GROWING LOCAL
MISSIONARIES

What Others Are Saying

"Wow! This little book is jam-packed full of practical wisdom. Dan helps us engage our world as agents of shalom, providing achievable steps to make a real difference in our cities and neighborhoods. I loved it!"

> **Deb Hirsch**, conference speaker for Forge (www.forgeamerica.com); church leader in Tribe of LA; co-author, *Untamed: Reactivating a Missional Form of Discipleship*

"'Seek the peace ...' no, wait, 'seek the SHALOM of the city'— blessing your place of exile. But how can we sing the Lord's song in this strange land? Drawing on years of experience in post-Christian Europe, Dan helps us answer this question. He invites us into a reflective process that moves us beyond the emotional shock of our transition into a new way of thinking and acting that benefits the cities and neighborhoods where God has placed us."

> **Leonard Hjalmarson**, adjunct professor, Tyndale Seminary and George Fox Evangelical Seminary; author, *No Home Like Place* and *Missional Spirituality*

"In the midst of the church's confusion and discouragement today, this book offers a lifeline of hope and praxis that actually works. Armed with a set of well-worn practices and a strong biblical framing, Dan helps the reader expand their horizons of imagination and engagement within their own community. This is a gem!"

> **Deborah Loyd**, founding pastor, The Bridge Church, Portland, OR; adjunct professor at Warner Pacific College; and co-creator of Women's Convergence

"Across the Western world, Christendom has been dealt a knock-out blow. *In Growing Local Missionaries*, Dan describes in practical terms what it looks like for followers of Christ to reach out, not with a theological right hook but with the hand of peace, offering hope to so many in our neighborhoods who daily live without it."

Dudley Callison, president, Christian Associates International

"I've been waiting two years for Dan to publish this exceedingly helpful book. Every Christian can learn missional behaviors that will impact their neighborhood for good and for sake of the Gospel. Great habits to change the world!"

Craig Williams, church planting strategist and associate, Presbyterian Centers for New Church Innovation, Presbyterian Church (USA)

GROWING LOCAL MISSIONARIES

*Equipping Churches to Sow Shalom
in Their Own Cultural Backyard*

Dan Steigerwald

Urban Loft Publishers | Portland, Oregon

Growing Local Missionaries

Equipping Churches to Sow Shalom
in Their Own Cultural Backyard

Urban Loft Publishers
2034 NE 40th Avenue #414
Portland, OR 97212
www.theurbanloft.org

ISBN-13: 978-1494761028
ISBN-10: 1494761025

Made in the U.S.A.

TABLE OF CONTENTS

ACKNOWLEDGEMENTS

I am indebted to many friends, near and far, for helping me acquire the insights and flesh out the practices described in this book. These friends include my fellow practitioners in Christian Associates (www.christianassociates.org), a community of missional pioneers and church planters in which I am privileged to participate. The list also includes my closer friends in Portland, Oregon, who on a day-to-day level walk out the missionary identity and lifestyle in ways that continually inspire me. And then there's my dear wife, Ann, who I have to mention, as she has been one of my deepest idea pools for the concepts touched upon in these pages. And last but not least, I am indebted to my "green team" comrades, who in many ways express a "Jesus lifestyle" more robustly than most Christians I know—Oh, if they would only discover the real Jesus behind the lifestyle! Thanks to all of you, for helping me lean into the vision, power and hope of shalom.

INTRODUCTION

This past year I downloaded an app on my smart phone that enables me to read the *New York Times* in doses all throughout the day. I love its in-depth news reporting on important or popular issues as well as the lengthy special interest stories. Occasionally, I come across an expose on some legitimate justice issue that seems poignant enough to post on my Facebook page. I figure there is so much trashy media pummeling our eyes and ears in every waking moment that it's worth affirming good journalism when I see it. Some people, however, seem to have problems with me calling out anything positive about the *Times*. Every now and then, Christian Facebook "friends" feel compelled to write nasty, pontificating responses to my postings. Their comments feel like accusations, as if they're suggesting I'm guilty of fraternizing with the enemy—the enemy, of course, being "those liberals." (I doubt they give a moment's thought to how my Facebook friends who don't follow Jesus see such spewing, and how they help fuel the stereotype that most Christians are narrow-minded critics.)

Yes, it's true that the *New York Times* is a "liberal" newspaper. And, yes, I know that most of the time they are not sympathetic or fair in their reporting on issues related to the church or to a Christian worldview. But come on! Why such strong, ungraceful reactions from some of my fellow Christians? Certainly, there are more factors at play than concerns about Dan sliding into leftist compromise.

In those moments when I'm tempted to be just as scathing in my own counter-remarks online, I remind myself that it's not really about me. I think such reactivity is actually symptomatic of a deeper unsettledness and anxiety many American Christians now feel. We are agitated when we see some of our more traditional stances on social issues being challenged— and even overturned—in the public sphere. We are angry that mainstream media often acts as though it holds the moral high ground. We feel anxious to find ourselves increasingly at the periphery of culture rather than at center stage. Put simply, it hurts to be marginalized or pushed to the side. (A recent Barna poll, by the way, suggests that this trend is on the increase in America's urban centers.)[1] So, when I consider the bigger picture of the Church's sense of estrangement from culture, I can see how liberal publications like the *New York Times* might be perceived as adding insult to the injury we feel.

Interestingly, while living and ministering among Dutch and expatriate Christians in Europe for 18 years, my wife and I encountered a similar hyper-reactivity toward the changes going on in the wider society. Unlike America, in The Netherlands and in the rest of Europe, the age and reign of

---

1 A recent poll by Barna, for example, shows America continuing down the pathway to a post-Christian ethos in her major cities. See https://www.barna.org/barna-update/culture/608-hpca#.UrDt3I0d748.

"Christendom"[2] on a societal level has truly ended. And this continues to be painful for Christians across that continent. The post-Christendom Church is now forced into rousing itself to create a new identity and way of operating in culture, simply to survive. This identity and way of operating has required, and continues to require, tremendous discernment, change and adaptation on the part of European Christians and churches. (We have yet to experience the intensity of this requirement in the States.) Some are moving on and finding fresh and positive ways to look at the challenges before them. But too many Christians, for various reasons, are still choosing a skeptical or pessimistic stance toward any progressive developments in wider society. They readily assume a resistive, even condemnatory posture, at any suggestion of participating with culture to foster the good of humanity.

When we left Europe and settled in Portland, Oregon, in 2006, you can imagine our frustration when we discovered so many of our Christian brothers and sisters displaying the same pessimism. Case in point: I was at a conference recently where I asked church leaders to share about how they get their bearings in the midst of all the unsettling changes happening in culture all around them. Everyone had great coping strategies that involved such things as trusting Jesus more resolutely, turning to the consolation of Scripture, and remembering that the Spirit is at work among God's people. But sadly, very few had anything positive to say about God's work and presence in the world. Most people seemed to be angry at the status quo, and full to the brim with gloom and

---

2 Alan Hirsch defines "Christendom" as "The standardized form and expression of the church and mission formed in the post-Constantine period (AD 312 to present), characterized by: 1) an attractional mode of cultural engagement as opposed to missional/sending; 2) a focus on dedicated, sacred buildings or places of worship; 3) an institutionally recognized, professional clergy class acting primarily in a pastor-teacher mode; and 4) the institutionalism of grace in the form of sacraments administered by an institutionally authorized priesthood." *The Forgotten Ways*, 276.

doom projections about the future. At one point I was so exasperated by all the despairing remarks coming from people's mouths that I threw my arms up and exclaimed, "Well then, I guess we might as well pack it up and go home! We have nothing to say to the anxiety all around us, right? If we ourselves have lost touch with hope, what do we really have to offer to the world God loves? If we truly believe that Jesus Christ reigns, that God by the Spirit is already giving us foretastes of the renewing of all things, how can we be just as anxious and despairing about the future as everyone else?" A silence fell over the room. But I could tell by the pained expressions on people's faces that my exhortation had hit home.

This attitude in the people of God, wherever encountered, is disturbing to me. I agree that we are wise to be shrewd and discerning as we address culture. Certainly, not all is good—on the contrary, way too much is destructive and opposed to Christ and the Way. But the all-too-common Christian response of criticism and negativism makes me wonder if we have a deep-seated identity problem. Are we allowing the changes in our cultural surroundings, the transitions pressing in upon us by this new post-Christendom era, to warp our view of who we are, of who God intends us to be? Are we merely victims in a world adrift, subject to the whims of history's unfolding, unable to do more than simply fight to survive? I fear we're so accustomed to the idea that we're bound by culture that our natural default is to see ourselves as captives or fugitives in our local and national settings. When we cast ourselves in such a negative light, is it any surprise that our approach to addressing culture is mostly negative (cf. Proverbs 23:7: "As a man thinks in his heart, so he is.")?

I think it's high time we show ourselves to be "in but not of the world" by exhibiting both a posture of godly conviction and also godly optimism—living as "resident aliens," if you will, instead of living primarily as "aliens." Among those who feel shackled or hemmed in by present cultural realities, and among those who have lost the ability to see opportunity in the midst of marginalization, I want to proclaim a counter message: Jesus _is_ trying to offer us hope and encouragement! Christ through the Spirit _is_ at work re-clothing and freshly empowering the Church with a fresh reminder of its calling!

I composed this little book because I want to add to the forces of hope that might help move the body of Christ into a more positive identity and upbeat engagement with the world God loves. With nearly every brand of Christianity beginning to wrestle with what "missional" or "mission-shaped" means when applied to church, it seems we are moving in the right direction. Our fellow-Christians in Europe are beginning to "put on" a re-invigorated way of being and acting in their worlds.[3] And, although quite a few American Christians are doing the same, we're in many ways still living in the abstract world of conversations and rhetoric about needed action ... while demonstrating little actual action.

Growing Local Missionaries is meant to be about real action— equipping people to move into the world with confidence in both their identity and their capacity to pass on basic missionary skills. As a starting point for this booklet, I've

---

3 The Church in Western Europe has had to respond to its own marginalization for many decades already. And yet the people of God are finding fresh opportunities for Christ as they learn to coexist in an arena of religious and philosophical diversity. During our time in The Netherlands (which might explain why I like the _New York Times_), we have seen those opportunities firsthand. In that faraway land, we observed a Church in many brands and colors trying to reinvent itself and find its new place at the cultural table. There are so many bright lights to note, so many Christians getting hold of another way to look at their situation. I think we have much to learn from our European sisters and brothers who are finding fresh ways to express the gospel and be the Church.

chosen one of the more profound stories in Scripture. It's a story about a tumultuous period in the life of God's people that I believe parallels, in many ways, the cultural turbulence we in the Western Church now find ourselves in. As you may have guessed, it's the story of Israel's exile in Babylon. This I'd like to use as a springboard to propel our interaction forward on two primary fronts: 1) helping us to shed any residue of the captive-prisoner motif we may be clinging to, so that we might embrace a much more positive identity for the times, and 2) equipping and activating us into a contagious, easy-to-pass-on, missionary lifestyle—a lifestyle that is already enabling many Christians to be agents of positive change in a host of different cultural contexts. As a co-learner and stumbling practitioner, I invite you to try on this new identity yourself. I also hope that you will find joy and Holy Spirit affirmation by experimenting with the lifestyle I'm proposing, as you yourself join God's mission within your own cultural backyard.

CHAPTER 1
EXCHANGING PRISON GARB FOR
MORE FITTING ATTIRE

Back in the early 8th century BC, God challenged his exiled people to adopt a new way of approaching an otherwise tragic situation. To accomplish this, he employed the prophet Jeremiah to speak into their immediate turmoil. This Word from the Lord was to come to the people in the form of a letter delivered from the homeland. It was an extraordinary letter, though its content would do little to alleviate the immediate culture shock they felt as they huddled in Babylon awaiting God's deliverance and vindication. The backstory that culminates in the delivery of this short letter is recorded in the book of Jeremiah, chapters 27-29. It is a story that I ask you to briefly enter into with me, as it helps set the stage for that opening crucial segment of the letter. That portion has much to offer in helping us live for God as we sojourn in the "strange land" we too find ourselves in today.

To briefly establish the context of these events, historically, they happened within an era where Babylon ruled on the world stage. This empire, under the iron fist of King Nebuchadnezzar, stretched far and wide, and sought to assimilate any nation and people who resisted its dominance. Any people who rebelled against this king were sure to meet serious consequences. Unfortunately for Judah, she chose the route of rebellion. She turned a deaf ear to the Lord's unusual request to submit to Nebuchadnezzar, and chose instead to put her confidence in an alliance with equally defiant neighboring nations. God's people heeded the assurance of false prophets, and found themselves judged by God, cast into exile, and depleted of hope and the means to resist.

Israel's "Culture Shock" and Echoes of an Ancient Calling

I want you to imagine yourself in the shoes of an exiled Jew in Babylon at this time. Your spirit is broken, your people have been humiliated and shamed and dispersed across a foreign empire. An unclean, barbaric people have desecrated the Temple, your holiest place, the symbol of God's veritable reign and presence. Your king and most of your religious and civil leaders have been dragged off to Babylon, and Nebuchadnezzar has installed a puppet king on the throne back home. You long for a prophetic message promising God's quick deliverance and judgment upon these foreigners you abhor. They deserve God's wrath to the utmost. In your fitful dreams at night, you vacillate between visions of sweet revenge and memories of the good old days back in the land of Judah. And you spend your waking moments in perpetual anxiety over what will become of you, your family and your people. The worst scenario imaginable has enveloped you and those you love.

And then ... the long-awaited Word of the Lord comes to you in your inconsolable misery. God has heard you! His vengeance and deliverance are at hand! Your ears strain to hear and comprehend its meaning, as it is read aloud among the ranks of your relatives and countrymen:

> Build houses and settle down; plant gardens and eat what they produce. Marry and have sons and daughters; find wives for your sons and give your daughters in marriage, so that they too may have sons and daughters. Increase in number there; do not decrease. Also, seek the peace and prosperity of the city to which I have carried you into exile. Pray to the LORD for it, because if it prospers, you too will prosper. — Jeremiah 29:4-7

While the meaning of these words is beginning to dawn on you, you hear still more words that warn you not to lean on the hope of false prophets—those who are promising peace upon you and upon your land back home. And with the warning comes the hope of a promise of eventual return: God will bring your descendants back to the land of Judah. His plans for you are to prosper you and not to harm you, to give you hope and a future. All this will come in due course. But not any time soon ... in fact, not for a very, very long time.

Continue to imagine yourself in the shoes of one of those exiles in Babylon on that very day you first receive the news. How would the news impact you as it sinks into your comprehension? In my mind, this kind of reaction would be quite normal:

> O my God, this cannot be true! You want us to do what?! ... Where is the promise of deliverance we hoped for, we prayed for, we need?! Where is the your hand of

judgment upon these wicked, brutal barbarians, who have desecrated your house?!

O, where now is our consolation, and where now will we find vindication?!!!

Tears flow from your eyes, wailing erupts around you, anger fills your heart. In your wildest nightmare, you never imagined God would be inviting you, his humiliated and broken people, to embed yourselves in Babylon over the long term. And worse yet, he is commanding you and your people to become an enduring positive presence and blessing to the most detestable of captors. This is HUGE! Praying for, serving, learning to love such enemies ... God, you must be joking!

Some, perhaps relatively few, hear the beginning of Jeremiah's letter and catch the echo of a familiar promise God made to Abram long ago:

> I will make you into a great nation,
> and I will bless you;
> I will make your name great,
> and you will be a blessing.
> I will bless those who bless you,
> and whoever curses you I will curse;
> and all peoples on earth
> will be blessed through you. — Gen. 12:2-3

Do you, reader, notice that echo in these verses? What words or phrases do you see that seem to allude to God's assurances to Abram (cf. also Gen. 17:5-7, where Abram is given the name Abraham)? In his tome, *The Mission of God*, Christopher Wright argues that the "increase in number there" (repeated twice), along with the promise of prosperity for God's people and for the Babylonian nation, echoes the very essence of the Abrahamic covenant. As Wright puts it,

There is something deeply ironic about this, since of course the whole story of Israel had begun with Abraham being called out of the land of Babylon-Babel. It might seem that history is going into reverse, with Israel being exiled 'from Jerusalem to Babylon' (Jer. 29:1, 4)—the opposite direction from the whole narrative of Israel thus far. But in the mysterious purpose of God, the descendants of the one called out of Babylon in order to be the fount of blessing to the nations now return to Babylon in captivity and are instructed to fulfill that promise right there. [4]

God intended Israel, for all its history as a people, to be an agent for the world's blessing. And that intention remained firm in the mind of God, despite the circumstances the exiles now faced in Babylon. Even in judgment (as this involuntary sending involved), God's exiled people were called to trust in his presence and plans for Israel among the nations. Their calling in the world was far wider than the tiny homeland territory they had left behind, which by now to them must have seemed like a distant dream.

Shalom for God's People AND for the World

Again, imagine yourself as one of those in captivity in Babylon. As you listen alongside your brothers and sisters in this foreign land, you happen to be one of those who capture allusions to the great covenantal promise God made to Abram long ago. Most of your people are so caught up in the immediacy of grief and anger over all that's happened that they cannot hear any echo of any hopeful vision at all. As you, among the huddled masses, strain to hear Jeremiah's letter,

---

4 Wright, *The Mission of God*, 99-100.

your ears also seize upon a word that has profound meaning in your native tongue—the word, *shalom*.

As we read the letter aloud today from our English translations of the Bible, it is easy for us to miss Jeremiah's (God's) significant word choice in what has become our chapter twenty-nine, verse seven. The NIV cited above, for example, translates the Hebrew text this way: "Seek the peace and prosperity of the city to which I have carried you into exile. Pray to the LORD for it, because if it prospers, you too will prosper."

What the NIV and most other English translations miss here is the repetitive use of the single Hebrew word: "shalom." In an effort to bring out the meaning of this word from the original text, our conventional translations interject words like "peace," "prosperity," "welfare," etc. Old Testament scholar Walter Brueggemann, accents the placement and recurrence of this word within the Hebrew text of our verse seven by offering the following translation: "Seek the shalom of the city where I have sent you into exile, and pray to the Lord on its behalf, for in its shalom you will find your shalom."[5]

By using the single word "shalom" three times in a single sentence, Brueggemann asserts, the Hebrew author intends to transmit some hefty meaning for the average Hebrew listener (or reader). To be sure, the concept likely rang out like a bell in the ears of the exiles hearing this portion of the letter read for the first time.

"Shalom" is perhaps one of the most significant, meaning-laden words in the Hebrew language. We see it and hear it, even today, such as in the famous priestly blessing that Yahweh

---

5 Brueggemann, *Living Toward a Vision*, 23.

Shalom, God Our Peace, instructed Moses to have Aaron pronounce upon the Israelites in Num. 6:22-26: "The LORD bless you and keep you; the LORD make his face shine upon you and be gracious to you; the LORD turn his face toward you and give you peace [shalom]." We anglophiles draw out only one facet of this word's profound range when we distill it down to the single word, "peace."

I invite you to take a moment to consider all that you understand to be inherent in that word "shalom." What does that word mean to you?

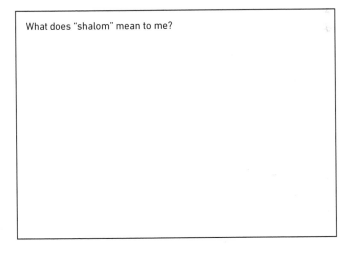

What does "shalom" mean to me?

So what would "shalom" mean to a Jew back then in Babylon (and perhaps even now, today, to a practicing Jew)? Perhaps you've captured some of this yourself, but Cornelius Plantinga defines "shalom" as: "The webbing together of God, humans, all creation in equity, fulfillment, and delight; universal flourishing, wholeness, and a rich state of affairs in which natural needs are satisfied and natural gifts are fruitfully employed, all underneath the arch of God's love."[6] Walter Brueggemann draws out the profound communal dimension of the word by defining it as a sense of personal wholeness in a community of justice and caring that addresses itself to the needs of all humanity and all creation.[7] Brueggemann and other authors I've encountered often allude to "shalom," in a biblical sense, as a visional term—the idea of people living now in the direction that God is moving all things. "Shalom" is about the future that's promised, but it's also about some measure of what God wants to give in the present (cf. "Thy Kingdom come! Thy will be done, on earth as it is in heaven.").

This little word "shalom," in the minds and hearts of the people of God historically, rang of community as God intended it to be. It echoed back to the perfection and beauty of Eden, and to the hope ahead of a new Eden on earth under the reign of the Messiah, where Isaiah's profound prophetic imagery of harmony comes alive:

> The wolf will live with the lamb,
> the leopard will lie down with the goat,
> the calf and the lion and the yearling together;
> and a little child will lead them. (Isaiah 11:6)

> The wolf and the lamb will feed together,
> and the lion will eat straw like the ox,
> and dust will be the serpent's food.
> They will neither harm nor destroy
> on all my holy mountain,"

---

6 Plantinga, *Not the Way It's Supposed to Be*, 10.

7 This is my condensed summary of Brueggemann's definition (see *Living Toward a Vision*, 181-183).

says the LORD. —Isaiah 65:25[8]

Through use of this word, and by indirect reference to the Abrahamic Covenant, God's people in exile were given the gift of a reminder of both their calling in the world and their hope for a bright future. But the application of this to their situation in Babylon must have been very hard to swallow. "Shalom," in all its hopefulness and consolation as a prophetic word, was meant to relate at that moment to a people they certainly hated. And its effective application in the sphere of Babylon would require the exiles to see themselves in a totally new light. More than that, it would require them to venture out into Babylonian culture, not as victims but as a pervasive force for good.

The Call to Put On a New Identity

We can now hopefully begin to see how extraordinary and challenging this letter must have been to those Jewish exiles in Babylon! God was asking his people to actively pray and seek shalom not simply for themselves, but for the cities of Babylon. And further, he was suggesting that their own shalom for the season ahead would somehow be tied up in the shalom the Babylonians themselves would experience. Take a moment to mull over how profound this challenge must have

---

8 One blogger I came across online put it this way: "Both of these passages deal with the kingdom age on the earth after the Lord Jesus Christ returns to reign on the earth as King of kings. The ferocious beasts (like the lion) will live peaceably with the gentle animals (like the lamb). Certainly, this will be a literal reality on the earth. However, this picture is also symbolic of the peace that will pervade the entire earth. When preachers speak of the lion and the lamb lying down together, they are referring to the time of peace when Jesus will reign as King over the earth." Reagan, "The Lion and the Lamb." That Kingdom Reagan alludes to has in some sense already come upon us. Jesus the King is now reigning and allowing the earth (and heavens) to bear witness and experience foretastes—even now—of that shalom reign. Shalom-sowing, whether back in Babylon or here in the 21st Century, is a prophetic and tangible pointer to the trajectory of all of history. So, when we use the word from this point forward, let us remember that it means much more than the simple word "peace."

been for a people who, for the most part, tended to see themselves as separate or a cut above all other peoples.

And, as you think of their situation in this new exile, imagine Babylon not as one diffuse and colossal megacity, but as a web of smaller towns and cities. God was exhorting his people not to view themselves as refugees lodged in short-term ghettos, but to view themselves as residents! For the long season ahead for them in this vast city, they were to assume a new identity far greater and more motivating than that of victim. Through this surprising Word from the Lord, Yahweh speaks a fresh and positive identity back into his people in captivity (the following is my rendering):

> You are NOT CAPTIVES in exile ... you are my MISSIONARIES OF SHALOM!

> My children, you need not wear the prison clothes any longer. Shed them, and dress in the garments of the ambassadors you are!

Can you see the vast difference between these two identities? It is hard to put a positive spin on the image of being a captive or prisoner. The other identity, on the other hand, is much more robust and positive—an identity which casts the people of Israel back toward their call in history, but also one that prophetically foreshadows an identity that Messiah Jesus would one day confer upon his people, the Church. Christopher Wright comments on the directives in Jeremiah's letter:

> I wouldn't have liked to be the messenger who had to deliver that letter and read it out to the exiles, because that is incredible stuff. Telling the exiles, these prisoners of war in Babylon, not to seek the shalom of Jerusalem (yes of course they were praying for Jerusalem all the time, that is

what Psalm 122 said), but Jeremiah says seek the shalom of Babylon, where you are, and pray to Yahweh for Babylon. That is incredible advice. In other words it is turning mourners into missionaries, it is saying you are not just to sit there singing Psalm 137, you are not just there to lament, you are there ultimately to be a blessing to the people that you live among. In fact, Jeremiah 29:7 is the Abrahamic mission directed no longer just to the nations in general, but to their enemies in particular. It is the closest you get to love your enemies in the Old Testament, pray for Babylon, seek the shalom of Babylon.[9]

I realize some may not agree that this letter fits within Scripture's general schema of God's mission to the nations, as missiologists like Wright and others contend. The point I want to make is this: In their particular situation of exile, God was challenging his people to shed their notions of being helpless captives stuck in a pitiable state. His was not a call to withdraw, nor was it a call to seek shalom only for themselves as a huddled people awaiting deliverance in a foreign land. Despite any instinctive urge they might have had to live cancerous lives in Babylon, infecting society with disorder wherever possible, God was supplying a counter-urge: "I want you to come in the opposite spirit and operate as visible, contributing citizens in every city where you are in exile. I call you to embrace another identity or way of being: you are my agents of blessing, my missionaries of shalom!"

God was asking the exiles to make a profound change in their self-perception. This would be the critical first step each Jew in Babylon would need to wrestle with. It would be impossible to sustain the long-term posture God was asking of them in the strange land unless and until they came to grips with this new identity.

---

9 Wright, "Prophets to the Nations."

And now I pose this question to us, to God's people lamenting over our own exile in Western culture: Could it be that God is challenging us to make a radical shift in our self-perception not unlike the one demanded of Israel so long ago? Our own trials in this hour may not be of comparable severity, but I believe the changes required of us are of a similar profound nature.

Our Call to Put On a New Identity?

It is not surprising that so many of us Christians in America feel anxious and even cynical when we consider the times we now face. Like our sisters and brothers in Europe this past century, we are being forced to walk through a blizzard of complexity and change that we have no control over. In the movement from Christendom to post-Christendom, European theologian and author Stuart Murray claims that the Church in the West is under pressure to make at least seven major transitions. Each of these represent significant changes that the Church in America also faces. Perhaps they are not yet as pronounced here as in Europe, but most of these transitions are already pressing upon us to some degree and will likely do so with greater force in the decades ahead.

Take a moment and consider how these transitions relate to you. As you read each brief description, ask yourself if that particular transition is presently bringing tension into your world or into the world of your church.

- From the center to the margins: in Christendom the Christian story and the churches were central, but in post-Christendom they are marginal.

- From the majority to minority: in Christendom Christians comprised the (often overwhelming) majority, but in post-Christendom we are a minority.
- From settlers to sojourners: in Christendom Christians felt at home in a culture shaped by their story, but in post-Christendom we are aliens, exiles and pilgrims in a culture where we no longer feel at home.
- From privilege to plurality: in Christendom Christians enjoyed many privileges, but in post-Christendom we are one community among many in a plural society.
- From control to witness: in Christendom church could exert control over society, but in post-Christendom we exercise influence only through witnessing to our story and its implications.
- From maintenance to mission: in Christendom the emphasis was on maintaining a supposedly Christian status quo, but in post-Christendom it is on mission within a contested environment.
- From institution to movement: in Christendom churches operated mainly in institutional mode, but in post-Christendom we must again become a movement."[10]

Whether you relate to every transition described by Murray or not, you would probably agree that cultural changes are pressuring us to change and adapt on a host of fronts all at once. We in the Body of Christ are in the midst of a long discernment over what we must hold onto as non-negotiable and what we must shed. It is time to let go of some antiquated ways of operating (including certain historical practices we should have never adopted in the first place).

The Jews were called to endure exile for a season, but their missionary commissioning in Babylon was consistent with

10 Murray, *Post-Christendom*, 20.

God's intention for them all along. They were to play a priestly function among the nations, representing the one true God while bearing witness to his love for the world in tangible ways. Did they fail God in this calling? In many respects, they did not achieve their wider priestly mandate. One thing we do know is that the people of Israel lacked the tangible presence of the Messiah, and arguably the empowering of the Holy Spirit as well. It is amazing to see their resilience and impact despite their limitations!

We the Church, in contrast to God's people in Babylon, stand on the other side of fulfilled prophecy regarding the Messiah, and we can declare with Messianic Jews everywhere: "For to us a child is born, to us a son is given, and the government ~~will be~~ IS on his shoulders. And he ~~will be~~ IS called Wonderful Counselor, Mighty God, Everlasting Father, Prince of SHALOM!" (Isaiah 9:6, altered to reflect fulfillment in Christ).

At the last supper before being betrayed to the Jewish leaders and the Roman soldiers, Jesus assures his troubled disciples with these words: "Shalom I leave with you, my shalom I give to you. I do not give you as the world gives. Do not let your hearts be troubled and do not let them be afraid" (John 14:27). And then on Easter Sunday evening, after his death, burial and resurrection from the dead, Jesus again visits his despairing and confused disciples, and once again he assures them: "Shalom be with you!" "Shalom be with you! ... As the Father has sent me, I am sending you. Receive the Spirit" (John 20:21).

Messiah Jesus, Prince of Shalom, has come! And he now leads his people, the church, into sowing shalom across the earth. And he does so in the power of the Spirit at work in the people of God. We are NOT CAPTIVES in our own cultural situation. We too, like the people of God dispersed across the towns of Babylon so long ago, are God's missionaries of shalom! We move out in a similar calling, and we move out with the empowering presence of God's Spirit at work in us, ahead of us, and through us![11]

Getting this across to missional leaders may be one of the most urgent priorities facing the body of Christ today. Not only do leaders need to apply this shift of thinking to their own lives, they need to also infuse it into the hearts of others under their care. This is no small challenge, as it constitutes a fundamental shift in identity from a negative, reactive, and fearful posture to a positive, faith-filled, exploratory posture. Imagine what could happen everywhere if we joined the Spirit to reinvigorate Christ's body with such a robust, positive identity and lifestyle!

When disciples of Jesus embrace their missionary calling, they are set free from the shackles of captivity-thinking to boldly step forward into their worlds—even into places where they never imagined God could be found! Like those initial bands of disciples whom Jesus sent out (cf. Luke 10), we are all called both to go out and prepare the way for Christ, but also to meet the people of shalom in the sacred places where God is already at work before we arrive.

---

11 In deference to those who would argue that the trauma of our present marginalization is not comparable to what the Hebrew exiles experienced, I would say this: Yes, it's true that our pain and displacement is fairly nominal in comparison to those horrendous early years the people of God faced in Babylon. But I would also argue that this story has much to speak to our present need to stop defining ourselves by what we are reacting against. Like our brothers and sisters of old had to do, we too must make a radical shift in our self-perception—from negative to positive. And also, as was required of those exiles long ago, we must learn to move across boundaries into the kaleidoscope of diversity that increasingly represents the culture of our cities. To me, this much parallels the great Exilic story of old, and we'd do well to learn from it.

As we sow shalom and as we form shalom communities, we bring tangible hope and healing to the nations. But that transformation has (and will continue to) cost us dearly. We must endure both the resistance and the wrath of the world (and I'm grieved to say, the "friendly fire" from within the church) in carrying out our commission. While it is upbeat and forward-moving, our call as missionaries is also deeply sacrificial.[12] As one culturally savvy blogger, Brother Maynard, once put it, what we offer is a disruptive peace:

> Shalom, is not so much "a peaceful, easy feeling." Establishing peace is a disruptive process. Hard to accept, the language of shalom is laced with political overtones and a call to extend blessing to those who wrong you. It is an announcement of the end of the age, filled with messianic metaphor and announcement of the Kingdom of God.[13]

This shalom commission remains ours as the people of God, today. In this tiny slice of eternity, we are called to be in and among nations, not "of" them (i.e., not held hostage to the world's damaging narratives about life and its meaning). Thank God for the tangible presence of the Holy Spirit with us and at work in us, or we'd certainly lose heart. I've heard many sermons about John 20:19-21, but very few about John 20:22-23. At the end of that great sending passage in verses 22-23, Jesus says: "Receive the Holy Spirit. [23] If you forgive anyone's sins, their sins are forgiven; if you do not forgive them, they are not forgiven."

---

12 Walter Brueggemann argues that the most potent symbols for the Church's call are the towel and the basin (cf. John 13:14). Unless we go down to the place of washing the feet of one another and the world, as Christ demonstrated, we will not be the people of shalom God calls us to be. *Living Toward a Vision,* 134-140.

13 Maynard, "Missional Order: Shalom."

We go out in the power of the Spirit to bear fruit in the world. And whether we perceive it or not at any given time, God's plans for the transformation of this world are right on track. God will not be thwarted. Nothing will stop his remaking of all things, and God will radically accelerate this in Christ's second coming. Shalom will one day prevail, and we get to play a significant part in the grand drama unfolding as missionaries of that shalom (not apart, mind you, from our role of announcing God's forgiveness of sins, a commission we must not take lightly). Now that's a reason to want to get out of bed in the morning and grab each day with gusto![14] (Note: We tend to skip over footnotes, but in this case, please have a look below at N.T. Wright's beautiful description of our shalom-sowing contributions for God in the here and now).

I invite you to pause for a moment and reflect on the following questions (on page 34). It's too easy to rush through these concepts with the mind, while not allowing ourselves the space to soul-search how deeply they really relate to us.

---

14 I love this N.T. Wright quote that validates our shalom-sowing contributions in this era, despite the overlapping of the present age and the age to come: "You are not oiling the wheels of a machine that's about to fall over a cliff. You are not restoring a great painting that's shortly going to be thrown into the fire. You are not planting roses in a garden that's about to be dug up for a building site. You are—strange though it may seem, almost as hard to believe as the resurrection itself—accomplishing something which will become, in due course, part of God's new world.

Every act of love, gratitude and kindness; every work of art or music inspired by the love of God and delight in the beauty of his creation; every minute spent teaching a severely handicapped child to read or to walk; every act of care and nurture, of comfort and support, for one's fellow non-human creatures; and of course every prayer, all Spirit-led teaching, every deed which spreads the gospel, builds up the church, embraces and embodies holiness rather than corruption, and makes the name of Jesus honoured in the world – all of this will find its way, through the resurrecting power of God, into the new creation which God will one day make. That is the logic of the mission of God.

God's re-creation of his wonderful world, which has begun with the resurrection of Jesus and continues mysteriously as God's people live in the risen Christ and in the power of his Spirit, means that what we do in Christ and by the power of his Spirit in the present is not wasted. It will last all the way into God's new world. In fact, it will be enhanced there." Wright, *Surprised by Hope*, 208-209.

Let me diverge for just a moment and speak again more specifically to those who are leading in the body of Christ. I am convinced that leaders in God's Church today need to come to grips with the importance of infusing this same sort of identity into the people they lead and serve. Leaders, however, must forego the temptation to think this doesn't relate to their own lives and discipleship. They themselves must sit in prayerful reflection over time, assimilating into their own spirits God's shalom and God's heart for the world. They must also recognize and own the reality of their own exile in Western culture, and learn to see ministry from the margins as an opportunity. They must acknowledge, in other words, that fighting to get back to some nostalgic past, where church leaders and their churches occupied a place of privilege and influence at the center of society, is not an option. And, of course, leaders must cultivate action out of this nurtured center of being, lest missionary living become an abstraction, something aspired to but not actuated as a sustainable posture.

Putting the Church's house in order is hard enough, but when you consider that we must also begin to think and act differently (and even become experimental on some fronts), it can all seem like it's too much. I actually encourage leaders not to press themselves into unrealistic timeframes as they introduce needed changes. Moving the church to embrace a positive identity and calling in the world takes time, energy, and intentional teaching and training. Church leaders must cultivate their communities as centers of shalom, and at the same time, equip their people to understand God's call to the local church to make disciples. That call means every single Christian participates in God's mission to the world as a missionary. Some will work out that call overseas, among unreached peoples, and through foreign justice/compassion initiatives. Most, however, will need to discover what being a missionary means, right in their own immediate neighborhood and city.

In teaching this material to various groups, I encourage leaders to teach on the concept of shalom, and also on those passages in the Bible that show the obvious workings of our missionary God (both his direct activity, and also his indirect historical activity through his people). I also encourage leaders to ask groups of Christians to whom they're introducing these concepts to process the following questions as table discussions:

- What difference could this identity make in my life and in the life of my faith community, if I (and most of my people) embraced it?
- If we live as missionaries of shalom, how would our non-Christian friends experience us, and what might that mean for our city?
- If we live as missionaries of shalom, what will it likely cost us?

Church leaders and pastors usually don't have too much problem generating vision and teaching related to the church's call to be on mission with God in the world. What they often lack, however, are practical handles on how to help people take even baby steps to act their way into a new way of thinking. As the ancient Chinese philosopher Han Fei Tzu tells us, "It is not difficult to know a thing; what is difficult is to know how to use what you know." From this point forward I want to move toward practical application, in order to give leaders (or actually anyone reading this) some handles on how to help infuse this missionaries of shalom identity into their church and other groups who have an allegiance to Jesus.

CHAPTER 2
ENGAGING AND ENRICHING
"BABYLON"

Getting Down to Practical Shalom-Sowing

So what would obedience to the Lord's command to seek the shalom of Babylon mean for the average exile, Jake and Sara? In seeking to answer that question, we are essentially probing into what it means, on a very practical level, to be missionaries. Every exile would have needed to adopt certain perspectives and behaviors in order to obey God's command.

Again take a moment and put yourself in the shoes of one of the exiles. Imagine some of the questions that would come into your mind as you begin to realize that you have to learn to do life in this strange place. Also, what attitudes and actions would you need to assume? I've put together a little exercise below to capture your thoughts. See what you can come up with—test your missionary sensibilities! Some initial clues lie tucked within Jer. 29:4-7, so train your investigative eye there first. Then set your imagination loose and think beyond what you see in the written word.

Exercise: What would seeking the shalom of Babylon require of the exiles?

Consider all the concrete activities and daily practices you and your family and friends would need to engage in to behave like positive agents of shalom. I have added a couple of examples, so that you can get an idea of some of the leading questions that the exiles surely had—questions that yield specific definable activities when we attempt to answer them.

OBVIOUS CHANGES SUGGESTED IN THE TEXT:

E.g. "Pray to the LORD for it ..." What would this require of me? Hmmm, definitely a daily choice to do this despite how I feel about these people. Right now I want to pray imprecatory psalms calling down God's punishment on all the Babylonians! I see my heart, and I need to move toward forgiving them. How might I adopt an attentiveness to God's leadings about my surroundings—how to pray, and eventually who to pray for? And what about praying communally for God's blessings upon my neighbors and city—how might I do that? What concerns do my neighbors have that I can bring to God in prayer, and how might I discover what those needs are?

OTHER (less obvious) CHANGES IN LIFESTYLE & PERSPECTIVE:

E.g. How can I relate to my neighbors when I don't speak their language or know their customs? Who might teach me? What has Babylonian society set in place to instruct newcomers like me in the language and ways I need to know to connect with people and learn my way around? What do people value here, and what are their cultural celebrations and observances, so that I might honor the ones that don't conflict with worship of my God?

How would I (and my people) seek the shalom of Babylon? Looking at the portion of the letter below and also using my imagination, what would that require of me?

> Build houses and settle down; plant gardens and eat what they produce. Marry and have sons and daughters; find wives for your sons and give your daughters in marriage, so that they too may have sons and daughters. Increase in number there; do not decrease. Also, seek the peace and prosperity of the city to which I have carried you into exile. Pray to the LORD for it, because if it prospers, you too will prosper. - Jeremiah 29:4-7 (NIV)

What did you come up with? How many clues were you able to dig out of the text? How many were you able to intuit or draw out using your imagination? Hopefully you found it helpful to get down to describing specific, concrete activities, attitudes and behaviors. If you found this hard, just think how hard it was for the people of God back then to imagine ways to move forward!

Missionaries everywhere struggle with similar issues and questions.

Here are some of the changes and behaviors that you may or may not have identified (and there are no doubt a good many more beyond these):

Obvious clues from the text:

- "Build houses and settle down."—I need to find work, venturing out to find materials, and also discover how the average citizen of Babylon manages life.
- "Plant gardens and eat their produce."—I have to do a lot of investigative work among the Babylonians about what grows in their climate, the harvest cycles, etc. I need to also get out into the countryside and city to find starter plants and seeds, including tools to till the soil and work the land.
- "Marry, have kids and find spouses for your kids when they grow up."—I need to become embedded in Babylonian society and do all that is required to create a stable long-term situation favorable to raising families. I must interact with the wider culture to find suitable spouses. But I also must stay true to my identity, while at the same time, let go of ever returning to an idealized separate existence.

Other activities we might imagine in order to move into Babylonian culture:

- I have to find a few people who can help me—i.e., other exiles who are learning the ropes, and specific neighbors I'm meeting who seem to be open or willing to help, etc.
- What appropriate activities can my kids participate in to get to know other kids and find needed instruction in how Babylonian society works?

- What business enterprises and civic enterprises might I join or create? (cf. Daniel, who eventually embedded himself as a leader in the civil affairs of Babylon).

These questions and the behaviors flowing out from them represent the sort of activities that missionaries have engaged in since antiquity. I like the particular requirement by God that the exiles proliferate shalom all across Babylon, as missionary work is often seen as primarily about evangelism, emergency response, and the building of needed infrastructure. Actively seeking to sow shalom (on a daily basis), and praying zealously for their host culture, would lead to a far greater overall impact than what is often the case with standard missionary work, even though proclamation and relief and development efforts are certainly vital aspects of seeking shalom for any area.

Over the long haul, as God's people consciously sought to integrate into Babylonian society as agents of shalom, we can imagine how significant they became to the prosperity of the city. And we can also imagine how many residents of the city came to see and appreciate the uniqueness of Yahweh. In an analysis of Henry Yoder's perspective on the exile,[15] Peter Leithart highlights Yoder's claim that the Jews' impact in Babylon was pervasive:

> Jeremiah's vision for Israel in exile was neither an effort to "Hebraize" Babylon ... nor a retreat from cultural engagement. Jews served the entire ancient Near East world as expert translators, scribes, diplomats, sages, merchants, astronomers ... Far from being a place of resignation and lament, Babylon itself very soon became the cultural center of world Jewry ... This is the cultural

---

15 Yoder, *For the Nations*, 51, 71.

and political program that the church inherited from Judaism.[16]

Today, as missionaries of shalom on the front end of our re-engagement with Western culture, we too must pursue similar kinds of creative, prayerful, and practical questions and behaviors as those many generations of exiles adopted. Is it too far-fetched to think that we too might eventually see the sort of impact Yoder describes above (as quoted by Leithart)?

So, where is your Babylon? Where has God placed you right now to live as an agent of shalom? How can you translate this same identity and lifestyle into your context as the Jewish exiles had to activate in theirs? And what is different now in this age where the Church is increasingly in exile, versus the age where Israel as a nation was in exile? These are critical questions, and hopefully I can answer some of them in the sections ahead. For now, let me start by suggesting an easy-to-grasp paradigm or pattern of missionary living that you can readily assimilate into your lifestyle, as well as pass on to others.

A Pattern for Missionary Engagement of our Neighborhoods and Cities

Most of the leaders and church folk my wife and I relate to want to respond to God's invitation to join him in cultivating shalom in their neighborhoods and city. They want to engage their own present-day Babylon, if you will. But often they lack the basic skills and principles of missionary living needed to actuate those desires.

---

16 Leithart, *Defending Constantine*, 294-295.

It is important to help churches bridge the gap and bring this call to mission out of the abstract and into concrete expression. Toward that end, I have devised a simple pattern of missionary living that is proving helpful in many cultural settings. The pattern is not prescriptive, but is meant to be descriptive of the normal behaviors practiced by missionaries as they embed and incarnate Christ within any given cultural set or subset. Such behaviors would have been practiced by the exiles in Babylon as they sought to fulfill God's command to seek the shalom of that foreign city. And those same behaviors, I would say, are activated already within any successful missional community or culture-sensitive church that has taken God's missionary charge seriously.

That pattern is defined by three couplets of action, with each couplet containing two present tense verbs (the singular words describing each couplet represent the end purpose that is in view and increasingly achieved as those actions are carried out):

- *Immerse and Listen* = absorbing
- *Connect and Befriend* = relating
- *Participate and Enrich* = serving

As we begin to explore this practical pattern, let me first emphasize that there is a natural sequence or order to the unfolding of these behaviors that quickly gives way to a repeating, overlapping cycle. When missionaries embed in a given setting, they must first immerse and listen, absorbing as much as they can about their target area. This observing and taking-in of critical information quickly gradates into relating or connecting with locals and those who are in-the-know about the area. Slowly over time, the relating leads to the building of a smaller subset of meaningful friendships, while at the same time it involves choices to join in and serve with locals in worthy causes or activities consistent with enriching the city. Any initial sequence soon gives way to a continuous, non-sequential engagement in all the missionary activities. With conscious attention to integrating these behaviors into daily life, they become habits individuals and groups learn to practice, almost unconsciously.

In order to visually capture and teach the ongoing, seamless nature of these behaviors in the lifestyle of missionaries, I depict them by employing a Celtic trinity knot. This knot becomes helpful to describing not only the continuous overlapping rhythm of these behaviors, but it also allows me to emphasize the importance of an ongoing dialogue with God and our spiritual community while practicing each couplet of behavior.

A Pattern for Missionary Engagement of the City

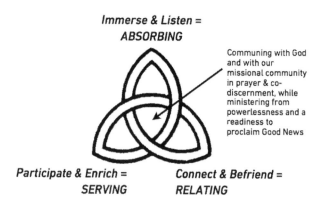

Immerse & Listen = ABSORBING

Communing with God and with our missional community in prayer & co-discernment, while ministering from powerlessness and a readiness to proclaim Good News

Participate & Enrich = SERVING

Connect & Befriend = RELATING

In the Celtic knot above, you will note that there is no beginning or end to the flow of the lines. Instead, a sweeping cycle of movements circles back and forth in a progressive but never-ending pattern (starting at the top, trace out the flow of lines with your finger, and see what I mean). The three verb couplets essentially operate in this fashion as revisited, overlapping dynamics that deepen over time. A missional group's initial plunge into context represents a starting point. But once the group dives in, the motion evolves into a repetitive rhythm of action that quickly leads to listening and taking in the surroundings, conversing with locals, and participating in the communal and social uplift activities of the host city. In that cycle of action the people of God ideally begin to experience a deep and meaningful comprehension of their context, a tactile interface with real and enduring friendships, and a communal impact that makes a difference for the Kingdom in their immediate area and city.

In the diagram above we can see that the rhythmic action always traverses the center, which I use to highlight the necessity of conducting all of our missionary behavior in continual interaction with the triune God and with our spiritual community. That central area I call the "zone of discernment." In order to see God's shalom manifest in the places to which we are called, we must remain ever-attentive to discern the harmonious voices of God, wisdom and experience—voices that can only be heard as we commune with the Trinity and with God's people on mission alongside us. This tethers our listening, conversations, and participation in culture to prayer and discernment.

As we step boldly into culture, we also "traverse the Center" in the sense of bowing to the reality of our dependence on the triune God. We do not come in the role of rescuers, but as ones who humbly lay down our power and quick solutions to allow God's wisdom and way to be discerned. This stance does not preclude the use of the gifts and experience we bring into a given context; but it operates against the backdrop of two guiding premises: 1) God's grace and power are often made most manifest in our weaknesses; and, 2) God's hidden potential and gifts need to be honored and awakened among those to whom we minister.

As we engage context and the people who inhabit our networks, we have to discipline ourselves to restrain our impulses to rescue and fix, as well as our tendency to promote dependence on our gifts and experience. We instead must seek to cultivate and magnify the potential already present in those places where we hope to see positive transformation. This takes time to learn and practice, particularly since we Americans idealize pragmatism and quickly default to relying on the experts to change things for the better. God's active presence precedes our arrival (referred to theologically as God's "prevenience"), and this should free us to explore the good that people are up to on a communal level, including those core motivations or longings God has placed in our neighbors as fellow humans made in the imago Dei (image of God).

Another cyclical motion through the God-Center of the Celtic knot involves discerning when and among whom it is appropriate to clearly proclaim the gospel (literally, "good news" in the original Greek). This is extremely important and must not be left out of our missioning. We followers of Jesus need to hear, comprehend, and be moved ever more profoundly by God's multifaceted gospel of the Kingdom. But we must also speak it and share it with boldness and sensitivity among those we encounter who have yet to follow Jesus. The Greek word from which we derive our word "evangelism" actually comes from the same root as the word we translate "gospel." They both connote "good news," so it is in some sense appropriate to say we are called as individuals and churches to "good news" (verb) our neighbors.

This good-newsing action certainly requires that we are lovingly embedding within those neighborhoods and subcultures to which we discern a call. But as Lesslie Newbigin asserts, if we are truly missionaries of God's shalom, we must not allow the unique ring of the gospel to be muted by all our good works and reputable participation in society:

> The congregation must be so deeply and intimately involved in the secular concerns of the neighborhood that it becomes clear to everyone that no one or nothing is outside the range of God's love in Jesus ... It must be clear that the local congregation cares for the well-being of the whole community and not just for itself.
>
> ... But, and this reminder is very necessary, this involvement must not become something that muffles the distinctive note of the gospel. The church ought not to fit so comfortably into the situation that it is simply welcomed as one of the well-meaning agencies of philanthropy.[17]

In short, we must share our conviction that God reigns, that a new day is at hand, and that the time is ripe for people to turn to him and trust his remaking of all things. In my estimation, evangelism simply involves that set of discerned, loving activities Christians engage in to provoke commitment to Jesus Christ in response to God's lavish offer of forgiveness and participation in the remaking of his world. As we commune with God and one another in dispensing our call to be "in but not of" the world, we grow in our capacity to speak and act in God-sanctioned ways that help people say "yes" to Jesus. We are privy to good news that unlocks the power of

---

17 Weston, *Lesslie Newbigin*, 145.

God, and people need to be given the opportunity to hear it and respond!

In summary, the Celtic knot is a profound image on which to hang the missionary lifestyle I am about to unpack in the following sections. It involves three couplets of dynamic practice, with our God at the center to enable us in the rhythm of practice to pray/discern with effect, minister from powerlessness, and proclaim the good news in winsome ways.[18]

---

18 If you want to do an early road-test on its validity in describing a missionary lifestyle, I encourage you to go back to your reflections on what the exiles would have needed to do in order to seek the shalom of Babylon as God instructed. Now classify each activity you listed with the associated end purpose that is in view: mark an "A" (for absorbing), an "R" (for relating), or an "S" (for serving). Some of those behaviors you listed will involve two or even all three of the primary missionary purposes or couplets. Again, as I said, this is a descriptive pattern of what missionaries do, and so it should not be odd that it works in application to exiles in Babylon, or Susan and Max in Portland, Oregon.

CHAPTER 3
MISSIONARY PRAXIS ON THE HOME FRONT

It is time we shed the negative images we have of ourselves. We are not prisoners or captives or helpless victims of contemporary culture. We are not an elite, a pure and separated class, intrinsically better than those not following Christ. We are not God's fist in the world, sent to enforce our values and lifestyles upon "nonbelievers,"[19] nor can we escape to that easy default posture of being cynics, complainers and criticizers. We, individually and communally, are commissioned to be missionaries of shalom to those around us and to our cities! And it is with some pressing urgency that we put on that mantle and get about the work God has given us to do in this world. But what does this involve on a practical level? What does it require of us to move out in this pattern of

---

19 I never liked using this word to describe people who do not know or follow Jesus. Everyone believes something, and a good amount of what people believe is consistent with the trajectory of God's Kingdom. To call a person a nonbeliever is actually dishonoring to the good they do believe, but it is also inaccurate as a description for non-Christians in general.

missionary engagement to actually "seek the shalom" of the neighborhoods and cities into which we are sent? Let's explore each of the couplets of missionary behavior that can enable any Christian or church to grow as local missionaries to their city.

Immerse and Listen – ABSORBING

When missionaries settle down among a specific people group or within a certain sector of a city, their first order of business is to submerge, to dip below the surface and absorb whatever data they can about their context. This "immersing" is akin to the experience divers have when they break the surface and peer into the wonders of a thriving coral reef. Only so much can be gleaned by observing from the boat, and much of what is seen from that outsider vantage point is either veiled by undulating waves or distorted by refracted light at the surface and below. But when divers plunge under the surface and join in the dance of marine life occurring everywhere above and within the jagged contours of the reef, they become not only observers, they become "participant observers." This means they enter into a posture of active absorption, where the live data of their surroundings is allowed to soak into their awareness. They probe, they poke, and they literally "swim in the same water" as the life forms they're observing do. And the participating, observing diver refrains from making evaluations, judgments or conclusions about the stream of information coming in, so that he or she remains receptive to new or unexpected information. They become what Peter Drucker calls "social ecologists"—ones who develop the ability to see the world as it is, not as they want it to be.[20]

---

20 Lenzner and Johnson, "Seeing Things as They Really Are."

Before Ann and I moved to Portland, Oregon, after nearly 20 years of living and ministering in Europe, we tried to prepare our young teenage daughters for the cultural transition ahead. Neither Ann nor the girls had ever lived in America, and what I knew firsthand of the culture was from a bygone era. So we explained to Andrea and Jenn that we were not going back to anything as much as we were going on ahead to our next missionary posting. As a family, we planned to approach our new environment in similar fashion to the way we had learned to integrate into Dutch culture and into the expatriate communities around Amsterdam and The Hague. We would plunge into Portland culture with the same curiosity and learning posture. It would be an adventure—a journey of immersion in a local neighborhood as first-time homeowners, meeting many interesting people, and taking in the beauty and secrets of the Pacific Northwest.

And so we made the plunge and broke through the surface. Because our oldest daughter wanted to continue the International Baccalaureate track she had started in The Netherlands, we decided to enroll her in Cleveland High School, an ethnically diverse school with over 30 languages represented among the student body. The choice of Cleveland High meant we had to actually reside within that school district, which limited our house search to the deep southeast part of the city. This choice narrowed the sphere of our initial immersion, and it gave me the opportunity to study the southeast part of Portland in advance of our final arrival in America.

Some Christian friends I had met on earlier trips to Portland cautioned me about living in southeast Portland. But the only part of the Cleveland school district that had affordable houses available was Brentwood-Darlington, a neighborhood that had earned the reputation of "felony flats." Evidently, there were methamphetamine production houses covertly spread across the area, and home break-ins were not uncommon. So the much-appreciated cautions from friends related to their concerns about how safe this part of town would be for my teenage daughters.

My initial "immersing and listening" in Brentwood-Darlington led me to believe that these concerns about drug use and crime were exaggerated. As I walked and drove up and down the streets of the area, I observed some evidence of crime and neglect. But I also observed a strong impetus toward rejuvenation of the neighborhood. Many single-family homes were showing signs of decent upkeep, and a good number had their own vegetable gardens and goats (this is called "urban farming," as I was to discover later). People were also friendly and down to earth, and most seemed to care about their neighbors and whatever social problems this area of the city suffered under.

After closing on an old home on a busy street with bus lines and bike paths, we quickly met our immediate Brentwood-Darlington neighbors. Some were overtly friendly and anxious to help us get situated. Others were reserved, unsure about how to relate to us. One neighbor, we discovered, was Danish, and within weeks she became a resource to us in bridging European and American culture. An elderly couple across the street welcomed us with flowers, and we discovered that 20 years earlier they had been missionaries in France! Such friendly folks proved to be great bridge-people, as they took the time to fill us in about the immediate area and its history.

As we ventured out into our neighborhood, we soon became not only observers; we purposely became "participant observers." We began to meet people by frequenting the local social hangouts—places like Papaccino's coffee café, the Laughing Planet diner, and various brewpubs (a Portland favorite for community, involving unhurried conversations over good beer). We also probed into the Christian scene in the city, and observed a great variety of churches. But we noted limited evidence of any of them really breaking the surface into non-Christian Portland. Most were reaching people who already had some exposure to a church or Christianity. Few were meaningfully penetrating into the huge group (40%-50% of Portland's overall population) who had little or no connection with the church at all.

Over time, through networking among churches and in the blogosphere, Ann and I managed to pull fifteen interested Christians together into a weekly home group to process how we might enhance our missional engagement with our southeast context. Each week we met over a meal in our home and wrestled with a particular question related to missionary living and its direct application in our lives. This helped propel all of us into deeper immersion and active inquiry about our city. We asked questions like: What are the needs of Portland on a social justice level? What healthy attitudes, behaviors and social patterns are evident in the city? What is its demographic spread in terms of ethnic, age, and socio-economic diversity? And, what are the obvious deficiencies and sins? (NOTE: I have included in the Appendices a synopsis of this simple missional small group we call "Missioforum").

Through this group and our own deepening network, Ann and I gained increasingly deeper insights into the Woodstock and Brentwood-Darlington neighborhoods and our city. We discovered that normal people all around us care about things we care about, and they were asking good questions, such as:

How can we remedy social and environmental issues via awareness and community action initiatives? How can we live more simply and in ways that counter consumerism? How can we honor and stimulate artistic and entrepreneurial expression across our city? Through other comments and questions we heard from neighbors, we also learned how caught up many people are in dysfunction and selfishness. How can we achieve America's notions of success and prestige? How can we "look out for number one" to ensure our own livelihood and prosperity? How can we medicate our fears and insulate ourselves against all the bad news we hear on TV about the economy, the environment, politics, etc.? These and many other discoveries helped us discern how we might best dovetail with local culture to begin to sow shalom and make a difference for good and for God.

As Ann and I work alongside our Christian friends, and as we have peeled away the layers of our Portland context these past years, we now hear more crisply the deeper cry of this city to rise to its idealism (so many I meet in Portland are supporting or participating in some great cause to change the world for good). And some of these cries have become our cries. Social woes like sex trafficking remain horrific in our city, and many people here agonize over how to reduce that terrible reality. Underemployment among a large class of young people, drawn to Portland's youthful artistic and altruistic verve, means that many live on the edge, without health insurance and often without much idea of where they will be in six months. These and other ailments plague our city, and we feel the pain of neighbors who suffer injustices often just below the surface. Immersing and listening is not simply a practice we perform in an emotionally detached fashion. It takes its own strong emotional toll as true solidarity with human pain always does.

As we (individually and in groups) immerse and listen in our city, we not only identify with people's hopes and pains, we also take steps to research the history and study the social vibes and rhythms of an area—where people hang out, where they shop, how they get around, what they do with their leisure time, who lives locally and who commutes, what is the ethnic and age demographic of given areas, what are the noteworthy landmarks and historic events and vices that contribute to making this place unique, and on and on. Such active inquiry requires us to be on the lookout for what is posted on telephone poles, on bulletin boards at supermarkets, on the windows of bus stops and communal hot spots. It means frequenting local "third places" (community spots beyond the primary relational zones of home and the workplace) to observe and innocently eavesdrop on the chatter around us, as well as strategically placing ourselves in various neighborhood advocacy groups or civic meetings. There are valuable insights waiting to be discovered every time we venture out. And these snowball over time into an increasingly deeper and more pervasive understanding of the uniqueness, beauty, and struggle of people and creation all around us.

As missionaries we must continually cultivate our listening and noticing capacities, comparing and contrasting what is already known about our context with new discoveries, while also taking stock of personal impressions and inner reactions to incoming "soundings." All the while, we stay pliable in terms of where the Spirit is challenging us to change, taking note of our discomforts, prejudices, judgments, and negative reactions to see what God would say and have us do about those. And at the same time, we note the positive turns in our spirit—the ways in which we feel drawn to or excited or energized by what we are hearing and taking in. I often recommend that individuals, teams, and churches create a running journal of their impressions, very concretely describing where they need to change, what they feel the Spirit is guiding them to pay attention to, and what key questions they have yet to explore.

I now invite you take a moment and consider your own practice of immersing and listening in that area where you live. Write a brief response to each of the questions below, and notice how readily you can answer them.

Reflections:
What are the pressing issues my city faces? What are the questions people are asking, and what needs and concerns do I commonly hear people talking about?

What seems to be good news to those God has called me and my church to be among?

What do my neighbors consider bad news, and where have I personally experienced the lament, pain and sins of the neighborhood or city?

Active listening requires cultivating an enduring receptivity, so that missionaries do not allow themselves to become like saturated sponges, unable to absorb new information and insights. My wife and I often recommend a number of practical ways to help keep missionaries in absorption mode. I'll briefly explain a couple of these below, as we have noted that many Christians and churches discover valuable insights through such exercises that help them discern ways to become better sowers of shalom.

First of all, we suggest that churches adopt some basic neighborhood listening rhythm into their community life. We use a particular half-day "exegesis" (literally, "reading out") exercise on a regular basis that continues to amaze us as to what it can yield, both in terms of information about an area and also in terms of enthusiasm among participants.

In brief, the listening exercise involves the following. Groups of two to four people venture out into a particular area of their city, armed with maps and a representative list of listening questions. We ask each group to set out in a different direction, to walk the streets and observe and process aloud what they are seeing. To deepen their observational stance (and add more fun), we ask and require each group to: 1) go into a local social hangout, buy a drink there and take in what is happening socially; 2) talk to at least one person; and, 3) bring back an artifact that captures, symbolically, what they have observed in their ninety-minute trek. When all the groups reassemble, we debrief by asking each cluster, one at a time, to share what they have seen, including any questions or inner reactions that emerged along the way. They end with a short story about their choice of artifact and how that relates to the turf they have covered.

When all the groups have shared, we ask listeners to reflect aloud on several questions, such as: What signs of the Kingdom do you see here (i.e., where God seems to already be at work)? What next steps might my church or missional team take to "seek the shalom" of this sector of the city? One of the best ways to wrap up the exercise is to have a subversive "insider" planted in the group, someone who actually lives in the area. As a closing act, we have that person respond to all that they have heard others report on. The insider almost always commends the groups for being fairly accurate in their observations, but their own story fills it out and helps everyone appreciate how much more there is to know about an area. This listening exercise is such a simple and effective teaching tool that we encourage churches to make it a repeating practice, so that a growing mosaic of observations is merged to paint an increasingly more accurate picture of a given area. (In the event that you want to try such an exercise with your own church, I include details in the appendix).

Another way to keep our listening sharp involves what we in Christian Associates call "the ministry of peripateo."[21] "Peripateo" is a Greek word often used in the New Testament to describe one's movement through daily life routines, literally meaning walking (*pateo*) around (*peri-*). We see a form of it used, for example, in Col. 4:5—"Use your heads as you live and work among (*peripateite*) outsiders" (NIV). Over several years, Mosaic Church of Glasgow, a Christian Associates (CA) church plant in Glasgow, Scotland, have made their "ministry of walking about" into a regular rhythm. Members of their core team regularly go out, individually or two-by-two, to walk and prayerfully listen, engage an occasional neighbor, and generally take in their city. What they continue to glean

---

21 This phrase and its practice actually originated with Dr. Wesley White, a CA missionary and founding pastor of Mosaic Church in Glasgow, Scotland.

through their prayerful listening helps the church both to keep their discerning ears sharp and also add to a growing base of knowledge about the city. These gleanings help the church to sustainably engage their city with the gospel, while also promoting the missional formation of those who join their faith community.

You may have encountered (or even developed on your own) some ways to help yourself and others remain in "sponge mode" as you venture out in day-to-day life in your part of the city or among a given population in the city. It's important to activate a regular practice of absorbing (immersing and listening), because there is no end to what we can learn about our surroundings and the people who inhabit them. This knowledge is key to our discernment processes, as we seek to discover how best to respond to what we're learning. Let us now move on to the next primary missionary behavior, which involves direct interface with those people who live and work and move all around us in our neighborhoods and cities.

Connect and Befriend – RELATING

Missionaries recognize that the people they encounter in their day-to-day wanderings are often the most immediately accessible resource for learning about their neighborhood and city. The second couplet of missionary practice, "connect and befriend," involves intentionally relating to locals who will open our eyes to the history and happenings in an area. It also involves cultivating no-strings-attached friendships with responsive people over time. These interactions involve connecting with both Christians and non-Christians, who in turn broker us into a deepening knowledge of and connectivity across an area.

As we, and those on mission with us, cultivate a host of connections, we can avoid reinventing the wheel by joining forces with other Christian insiders who are already embedded. God has seeded our city and the local body of Christ with scores of fellow Christians who possess apostolic, prophetic, and evangelistic gifts (cf. Eph. 4:11). These folks are often well-networked, and they naturally propel people into cultural engagement. Their outward orientation enables them not only to identify the patterns, structures, and sins present in society that harm people, but they also can be effective advocates who unite concerned parties (both Christian and non-Christian) to turn such negativity around.[22]

Many established churches also have a long partnership with neighborhood and citywide community development efforts, and we are wise to cultivate relationships with these churches. I will say more about the issue of cooperative venturing with other Christian groups later when discussing the last couplet of missionary behavior, but I highlight the need for such alliances here, as too many missionaries undervalue what they can learn about an area or people group from local pastors and ministry leaders. Or they avoid church leaders because too many pastors are antagonistic to missionaries operating in proximity to their churches.

Obviously, some of the most important connections we can make in a new setting involve our relationships with locals who do not see themselves as Christians. They, after all, represent the primary reason we are coming into a given setting as missionaries. Unfortunately, for too many people in the Church, relating to these kinds of everyday people does

22 For more specifics on what these "APE" orientations constitute, I suggest Alan Hirsch and Tim Cathcim's excellent book, *The Permanent Revolution: Apostolic Imagination and Practice for the 21st Century Church* (San Francisco: Jossey-Bass, 2012).

not come naturally. And when we challenge such Christians to step into these kinds of relationships, we are often met with resistance.

Yes, the unfortunate reality is that far too many Christians do little or nothing to cultivate relationships with people outside the Church. When I converse with Christians in Portland and other cities, they commonly admit to not having a single significant relationship with a non-churched person. This disturbs me, but it does not surprise me. What still does shock me, however, are those times when I meet Church leaders (and even some aspiring to start new churches!) who are not able to tell me the name of one non-Christian person they know as an enduring friend. I am convinced that a big part of the Church's missional formation across America must now involve getting back to the most basic level of motivating and equipping Christians to have natural relationships with normal people! That is a pretty startling reality.

I recently read a blog entry written by my friend Dave DeVries that captures the struggle that we as Christians have in relating to non-churched people all around us. Dave cites an article he read called, "Why People Struggle with Engaging a New Culture." In that article, the author cited the following reasons why people hesitate to cross a cultural boundary, and you can see how they might apply to us as we relate to non-Christians. As you read them below, including Dave's commentary on each, take note of the reactions you see in yourself at the prospect of needing to step forward to engage non-Christians.

- *I don't want to.* This response may take a variety of forms from "cocooning" in your own home instead of meeting your neighbors, or only spending time with your Christian friends. This may be verbalized directly, or simply observed through busyness with "church" activities.

- *I don't know the culture around me.* This lack of basic cultural awareness may result in avoidance or resistance to actual engagement with the people and places around you. Failure to understand and appreciate the culture will prevent healthy missional initiative.

- *I don't like the culture around me.* This is clearly related to the above perspective that lacks an understanding of the culture. Failing to make friendships with those who live near you in the culture may lead to a strong dislike for the culture. Maintaining a distance from the culture in turn leads to a posture of judgment rather than understanding. Even when you dislike certain aspects of the culture around you, building relationships with people within the culture can open your eyes to appreciate differences.

- *I'm afraid of cultural differences.* Oftentimes when exposed to different cultural behaviors, there is a sense of fear that results from the unknown aspects of the culture. We're often afraid of things that we don't know anything about. This may appear as feeling disloyal to my own culture and my friends. It may also be reflected in viewing cultural differences as wrong rather than as simply different. Again, encouragement and friendships are key to adapting to and accepting cultural differences.

- *It doesn't feel right.* From a personality standpoint, the more rigid you are or the more structured you may be, the more difficulty you have in a new environment. Making cultural adjustments can be challenging wherever you are. While you cannot change your personality, being aware of who you are can help you to identify why things don't feel right. Personal awareness can help overcome resistance to engaging the culture because "it doesn't feel right."[23]

---

23 DeVries, "The Challenge of Engaging Culture."

I have lived many years in international settings myself, and I know too well the power of every one of these reactions when faced with crossing a cultural boundary. It is much easier and more comfortable to relate to people who speak our language, share our values, and practice our way of life. When we venture out beyond the safe haven of our familiar church culture, and as we enter into the social networks of non-churched people, we should not be surprised to see these kinds of reactions welling up in us. And we should not beat ourselves up for reacting negatively. What we do with those attitudes, however, is very important. When they become rationalizations to excuse our continued separation from people who do not know or follow Jesus, then we have a problem. Finding a "missional coach" to help us overcome our attachment to a church-centric way of life may be our best step forward.

For whatever reason, many church leaders seem to have lost the will and ability to activate the body of Christ into a meaningful interface with the very world that Christ died to reach. Connecting with and befriending non-Christian people takes deliberate, repeated actions to become a sustainable practice in the life of a church. And to the extent that we as leaders can describe those actions concretely, model a few ourselves, and release coaches experienced in missionary activity, the church's missional formation will be greatly enhanced.

When we concretely describe the actions that lead to befriending normal people in our networks, this often helps people get handles on how to move forward, while also showing them that it is not as difficult as they might think. I often encourage my church friends to look for opportunities to join or establish an affinity or common interest group among non-Christians in their networks. But I never suggest that without first asking them to do a self-inventory of what they are passionate about or interested in, including where they are already naturally activated on a social level. It is easier to initiate and sustain group involvement if we enjoy a given activity (e.g., sports teams, yoga classes, classes, etc.).

To enhance our natural connectivity with non-Christians, we can also choose a popular community space to frequent regularly, such as a coffee shop we like or a restaurant or business we particularly appreciate. Missional author Mark van Steenwijk reminds us that third places (like Papaccino's mentioned earlier) can be fertile zones for what he calls "intentional friend-making":

> "Intentional friend-making" is different than "friendship evangelism" because the goal of friendship evangelism is to share your faith with your existing friends. I highly encourage that. That is a great thing. But the problem is that if we stop there, we never move beyond our (usually homogenous) circle of friends.

> Here's the basic idea:

> Pay attention to where people congregate and hang out. It could be a coffee shop, it could be a bar, it could be the park, or the library, or a cruddy diner, or the local YWCA, or community center. We should try to spend our time more and more where neighborhood people spend their time. This won't work as well in suburbs, because people don't center their lives in "third places" in the suburbs— though many do in urban and rural places.

> It isn't enough to spend time there, though. You must engage people there. This is where it gets sticky for people. We don't naturally make friends in public places like that, though it is socially acceptable to do so. Many people hang out in "third places" because they want to connect

with a neighborhood and their neighbors. These are the general rules of social interaction that I have discerned:

1. If you see someone at your favorite place a few times, you have permission to give them the "nod" of recognition (or subtle wave).
2. If you've recognized their presence a couple times, it is socially ok to say "hello."
3. Once you've said hello to someone once or twice, it is ok to make comments like "hey, it sure is nice today" or "is that book you're reading interesting?"
4. After you've broken the ice, you can introduce yourself.
5. Once you're on a first-name basis. You have social permission to have normal conversations with them, and things develop from there.

Here's the thing: most of us follow this sort of interaction in settings like school or at church, and it is perfectly normal there. Just realize that it is ok to do those sorts of things at third places too. If you are a bolder person, you can skip steps. It isn't offensive to have polite chit-chat with strangers. It is only rude if you do it when they are in the middle of something that requires attention. Even then, most people won't decide you are a jerk, they'll probably just think you're a ditz. And that is better than not knowing them at all. Those of us who make connections with people in this way will be able to graft them into our network of friends. So in a healthy church, only a handful of people need to be doing this well for the whole church to be making new friends.[24]

Australian author and evangelist Michael Frost offers helpful input on what it takes to build friendships with non-Christian people. Frost says that three primary ingredients are needed: 1) creating proximity (i.e., nearness) with non-Christians; 2)

---

24 van Steenwijk, "Incarnational Practices."

being willing to meet frequently with them; and 3) being willing to prioritize our relationships with them so that we can more spontaneously meet or talk when they want to meet or talk. To season our lives with these ingredients is costly! It means we have to create room both in our schedules and in our relational pools to accommodate new people that are quite different from us in values and lifestyle. How many of us are willing to work that sort of flexibility into our schedules, especially when it may mean reducing our commitment to church programs and church meetings?

Reflections:
How do you yourself prioritize the building of friendships with non-Christians? (Remember, you will often discover shalom for your own soul as you consciously seek it for those who do not yet know Jesus.)

How might you and your church create "belonging spaces" for non-Christians who show an interest in spirituality but are not yet ready to step into a church environment?

Is there anything you could do in your life or church to enhance connection with people outside the church? What measures or steps will you take to make this happen?

To mobilize this connecting and befriending practice, Ann and I often challenge our Christian friends to get into the habit of practicing simple hospitality. Extending hospitality can bridge relational distance and quickly turn strangers into friendly neighbors. And having people over for dinner or for a film or game night can go a long way in creating the sort of belonging and conversation spaces non-Christians need to begin to hear and believe our Story. This invitational practice, however, ought to get beyond home hospitality. I think it is critical that we learn to be hospitable people wherever we go. To carry that in ourselves means we grow in our capacity to convey approachability, interest in, and attentiveness to, normal people. The more we relate to non-Christians in this way, the more we are able to reduce our visible cringing at the muck and sin and language and selfishness we encounter in their lives—keeping in mind, of course, that we have our own muck and sin and other fruits of selfishness to keep at bay. Conveying acceptance to our friends, by the way, does not mean condoning their choices, but humbly keeping to ourselves our judgments and recognizing our own acceptance by Someone willing to be patient and longsuffering with us.

Not long ago this was put to the test in my own journey. I was given the opportunity to re-establish ties with a dear friend I grew up with, a friend who had intentionally removed himself from my circle of relationships for nearly twenty years. Mark (not his real name) had moved far away from our hometown in his twenties, and had in the meantime established a booming bar and restaurant business. I long suspected that he was gay, and I wondered how much his estrangement was the product of fear of judgment from his family and friends. When I was new to the faith, I had been pushy and preachy with Mark in ways that suggested I was anything but a hospitable person. For years this bothered me, as the last thing I wanted to do was damage my relationship with this valued childhood friend.

Several years ago, Ann and I were invited to a conference held at a venue not far from the town where Mark operated his restaurant. I decided to call him and ask if Ann and I could come over to visit him for several days. All my earlier gestures to re-establish relational ties had been met with only lukewarm responses. But this time, to my surprise, Mark was enthusiastic about the idea, and even offered to host us in his own home. When we arrived at his house, he and his long-term partner warmly greeted us and invited us into their world. As we vacationed with Mark and his partner, and hung out at the restaurant with his friends, I began to see Mark and his lifestyle in a new way. I saw how committed he was to his partner, and how caring he was in general toward others. And I heard stories from Mark's friends, which helped me to understand some of their dreams and a bit of their pain.

During one of our visits to the restaurant-pub, I recall sitting at a table some distance from where Mark was standing. Over the drone of live music playing in the courtyard and numerous wide-screen TV's broadcasting live sports, I could hear him proudly bragging about his friend, Dan, being "a minister who travels the world to help people everywhere." Later that evening, Ann and I were sitting in the upstairs bar talking with Mark and his gay friends. As more friends arrived, Mark was quick to remind them that I was the minister guy he was referring to earlier. In the midst of all the friendly chatter, one of Mark's friends, ornamented to the hilt with gold jewelry and makeup, suddenly stood up and said rather loudly, "Can I kiss you?" Immediately, I felt a recoil reflex rising inside me as he moved toward me. In that moment I prayed silently for

God to help me not to react and run! I managed to stand my ground unflinchingly, and I turned my cheek to receive a kiss that I knew came out of both genuine respect but also out of a desire to test how I would react. The man returned to his seat, and conversations resumed. Thank God, I did not move away. The next morning you can imagine my joy when Mark told me how positive an impression I had made on his friends during our short stay. By an act of grace beyond me, I had in some small way reflected God's hospitable nature. And an old friendship has been revived.[25]

Missionaries learn to see themselves in solidarity with their human family made in God's image, and they take pains to relate with them as friends and fellow journeyers in need of deeper meaning and purpose in life. And in relating to non-Christian people, we begin to recognize that God was already at work in their lives before we showed up. We discover that they too have longings and deep yearnings for wholeness, justice, and acceptance, as well as for experiencing beauty and creativity and joy. And at times, God will also use them as vessels to minister deeply to us—an avenue of blessing that too few Christians ever think to open themselves to and access.

As we practice the initial missionary behaviors, diving in deeply and absorbing critical information and impressions about our surroundings, while also relating to locals and neighbors, we begin to see ways we can plug into good causes and initiatives all around us. The motions we take to join in

---

25 I am still wrestling with how to reconcile the biblical narrative with the gay issue, especially as that pertains to long-term, non-promiscuous, committed relationships. At present I have trouble seeing these as "normal" in light of the trajectory of God's shalom Kingdom. But we live in an in-between age, where brokenness means many things are not operating according to normal design. There are anomalies that do not seem to fit in the category of "sin," and perhaps these committed homosexual relationships fit that category. In any event, I want to respect all Christians who wrestle with Scripture and in good conscience arrive at a different place on this issue.

and serve alongside are what Ann and I call the practice of "participate and enrich."

Participate and Enrich – SERVING

Local missionaries will be vigilant to join existing shalom-sowing initiatives in their city, and they will join hands with others in creating ones that do not yet exist in the area. It is important to remember that we are not simply trying to be missionaries, but we are aiming to be missionaries who, in the spirit of Jeremiah 29:7, intentionally provoke and bring shalom. Embedding in culture; becoming familiar with the way locals view the world and live their lives; and even sharing the Good News in creative and sensitive ways—these are all great. But an even deeper and more profound interface can happen when we take action with both Christians and non-Christians to express compassion, pursue justice, and restore beauty right in our own neighborhoods and city. Participating in culture in these ways eventually leads to an enriching of context in some way, with signs of shalom tangibly evident.

To aid our participation with others in shalom sowing, again I reiterate the importance of enlisting those Christians we know who move in apostolic, prophetic and evangelistic giftedness. As we try to walk wisely and shrewdly into the muck of society, these types can help us discern how the damaging narratives and behaviors of our city might be resisted and overturned by alternative (ideally, gospel-centered) ways to live. We can then enlist both Christians and non-Christians to come in the opposite spirit to address the patterns, structures, mindsets, and sins that diminish or destroy people God loves (and who hopefully we are also beginning to love).

"Participating and enriching" as a missionary activity can lead to remarkable impact across an area. But it is important to draw attention to another benefit it provides, and that relates to our personal discipleship. Our missional activity with others changes us! We comprehend the gospel in deeper and deeper ways as we serve with others, our faith is often deepened by the ways we witness the Spirit at work, and we gain handles to explain different aspects of the good news to our non-Christian friends serving alongside us. I often tell my Buddhistic carpenter-friend that he is living a Jesus life better than many Christians I know; he just lacks the critical piece of knowing the One who is behind his own impulses for good – Jesus!

In our busy lives, as we endeavor to sow shalom with others, we have to be careful to monitor the load this puts on us and on others we enlist. Rather than simply heaping new missional activities upon already challenged schedules, we need to be discriminating about what we can realistically take on. This requires discernment and sensitivity to God's leading, but also an activating of our own natural areas of interest where possible. Much like the hobbies and interests we naturally pursue, if we serve in justice and compassion initiatives for which we already feel a burden, these are much more likely to become sustainable practices. Churches often miss this when they choose service trajectories in culture that disregard the natural passions of their members. Part of a collective missionary posture means church leaders take an inventory of the passions within their church and correlate those with discerned areas of need and opportunity in the city. (The other side of this coin, of course, involves taking an inventory of what community development workers call the "assets" already resident in our city.)

In my own life in Portland, Oregon, I work alongside a group of eco-enthusiasts. This has been a huge blessing for me, as I have long desired to increase public awareness and involvement in creation care. My deep affinity for nature, wildlife, and woodlands beauty dates back to my childhood and was immediately reignited when I stepped into the cathedral of the Oregon outdoors. I decided to check into local options for eco-activism as both a way to activate a core passion and as a way to meet people as a newcomer to the city. In my search I stumbled upon the "Master Recycler Program," an eight-week cohort experience aimed at equipping participants in the knowledge and practice of recycling, reducing waste and consumption, and reusing existing goods and materials. I signed up, finished the course and its thirty-hour community service requirements, and soon fell into a rich network of local eco-sensitive, community-minded folks. Some of these were Christians, most of them were not, but all of them showed a deep concern about many of the things that I believe Jesus is concerned about: honoring and caring for our neighbors, pursuing simpler lifestyles, helping people see their responsibility toward and connectedness with creation, etc.

I can honestly say the Master Recycler Program was the best $50 I ever invested! That badge has opened doors for me to serve around the city at recycling and collection events, farmers' markets, neighborhood surveys, community gardens, neighborhood cleanups, tree plantings, etc. More importantly, it has enabled me to unite with twelve or so neighbors to foster the cause of creation care and simple living. We refer to ourselves fondly as "the green team," but we are really a collection of well-traveled, free-thinking social activists who have learned to appreciate one another's uniqueness and common values. After five years of doing special environmental and sustainable living projects together (including drinking lots of good beer and sharing many meals together), Ann and I now enjoy the richness of these special friends. None of these folks would claim to follow Jesus, yet shalom is being sowed through the care and service of our little missional community. Our friends know that Ann and I are Christians. We have not hidden that, and at times it has produced some mild friction and lively conversations. But I feel free to be who I am, to serve alongside these folks as an act of worship to Christ, and to simply be a friend who stumbles forward in caring and listening and loving.

And so, as you can see from my own little slice of experience, participating and enriching can readily happen at the intersection of natural passions and the felt needs of our local context. We can cultivate human connections into friendships in organic, natural ways (forgive my eco metaphors) as we do worthwhile activities together. And we can be free to live out our story in the light of the grand Story, acting as salt among those not following Christ, while also not making our emerging friendships dependent upon what they do with Jesus.

This salt-seasoning of shalom-sowing communities, of course, can be greatly enhanced by including other Christian friends of like sensibility. I continue to look for other local Christian friends to join me in various projects our green team is undertaking. This helps increase the interface my non-Christian friends have with my Christian world, which hopefully allows them more opportunities to both experience Christ and also to diffuse their negative perceptions about Christians (i.e. maybe Dan is not an anomaly, and maybe there just might be more caring "green" Christians out there). But even apart from enhancing proclamation, it makes sense to include my Christian friends, because they help me stay true to what I believe and mindful of the opportunities to pray for and love this group of people who are not presently following Christ.

One simple way to include other Christians in our daily interface with locals is to schedule our meetings out at popular community watering holes (some call this "mobile office-ing"). You never know what might ensue when "two or more gather in Christ's name" at places our local friends and neighbors frequent. This reality was driven home to me again recently as I met with a pastor at Papaccino's, the local coffee hot spot I've mentioned earlier. Both of us were so surprised by the natural, unprovoked interface we had with one of my non-Christian neighbors that I rushed home to write the following letter to encourage my Portlandia missional friends:

> Hey guys, thought you'd all appreciate this little story, esp. since some of you met my neighbor, Tony, at our Centennial house party in early September.
>
> I scheduled my first coaching connect this morning with Longview pastor, Ryan Snowley. (Ryan is part of the new ForgePDX missional training cohort, and we met at Papaccino's so that I could fill him in on the 2 recent gatherings he's missed). When I entered Papaccino's, I immediately spotted Tony sitting in the corner reading the paper, with another guy sitting next to him sipping coffee and texting on his phone (turns out this was Ryan, whom I had never met F2F). I greeted Tony, and he cheerily returned the greeting with, "Hi Dan, fancy meeting you here this morning!" Ryan of course picked up on the name association, and bolted upright, hand outstretched, and said, "Hey, you must be Dan Steigerwald." I said, "Yes, Ryan, that's right. And this is my neighbor, Tony." After a cordial nod to Tony, Ryan sat down, and then Tony, being the social talker he is, says, "So what are you guys getting together to talk about, since

you're obviously just meeting each other for the first time."

I explained to Tony what this man, Ryan Snowley, is doing as a pastor among some of the poorest folks of Longview, WA. I mentioned further that Ryan and I were getting together to talk about how I might help him and his church be more effective in serving this group and being an agent for good in his city. Tony knows I do coaching, and he saw that we were ready to get down to business. So he smiled, and picked up his paper and pretended to be reading, though I knew he was in earshot of everything we were about to process…and he was listening.

Ryan and I jumped in and talked about the state of American society, including both the bad and the good on how the church tends to relate to culture. To Ryan's credit, he didn't resort to religious, churchy-land language, and we started doing a passionate back and forth exchange about what's missing in the church's equipping and how the good news often gets masked when churches are mostly about providing religious goods and services to their members. Knowing that Tony is an intellectual and is big on the idea of meta-narratives, I talked (loudly) about Christ's story and our need as Christians to be true to our story, while also mentioning our need to be interactive in a no-strings attached servanthood manner with our local neighborhoods and social service organizations. Ryan piped in some comments about teaching people to do evangelism in ways that seek friendship and not simply focusing on letting people know that they need to stop sinning and be morally upright so they can get to heaven. And so the conversation unfolded …

We talked robustly about such things, and about what the ForgePDX cohort involves. I pulled out the 3 books I was about to pass on to Ryan, and explained why we chose these particular books (noting out of the corner of my eye that Tony was peeking and clearly following the conversation). And on and on this went, for 45 minutes, when Tony suddenly stood up and announced that he needed to get going. While throwing his jacket on, he looked at Ryan and me, and said, "Well, it sounds like a superb interactive process you guys have got in mind to get at those three themes of cultural shifts and new paradigms, sustainability"—though I think Tony was thinking a green agenda—"and leadership." He was clearly listening behind that newspaper, but even more, he was taking mental notes!

And then, this sweet ending ... Tony says in parting, "Well, I'm not part of any particular sect myself, just trying to be part of the greater good." And I interject without pause, "That's nonsense, Tony," you're part of the sect of the pax Americana, whether you want to be or not. We're all part of bigger stories, and we interact with each other and our cities, for the common good ... and actually sects don't do that." Tony says, "Hmmm, I guess you're more like a tribe than a sect? And I'm just part of the bigger tribe that wants to find common ground for many different tribes to work together." And I say, "Tony, this is a big part of why we're offering the training Ryan and I are talking about today—it's because we believe that too, just like you." Tony then gives us a big white-teethed smile, and he heads for the door.

I appreciated the Spirit's work in this encounter for these reasons. For one, this was the best way for my dear neighbor, Tony, to hear more about what I stand for, including my stance on Jesus, the church and the gospel. Because Ryan and I had a scheduled meeting, Tony knew it was not appropriate for him to be his talkative self. He was bracketed by circumstances into the role of a listener, and I think he heard more in 45 minutes while fake-reading his paper than I could have hoped for in any prolonged, direct conversation with him over the backyard fence. He simply interrupts too much, sidestepping the conversation with his opinions on everything. Secondly, this encounter provided an object lesson for Ryan and I to dissect after Tony left. In short I was able to bring Ryan up to speed on what he missed in the last two ForgePDX gatherings by relating that material to the experience we just had with Tony. The Spirit helped create a teaching moment, and I could see that Ryan was really "getting it" to the fullest extent.

This was a surprising, superb coinciding of lives and stories that I wasn't expecting, and I went away on my bike smiling in thanks to God!

Never underestimate what God is already up to when we innocently walk into a coffee shop to engage another missional friend ...

Shalom to you this day, and always,

Dan

Exercise:
Make a list of the natural passions and interests that you have.

What group, initiative, etc. might you join to sow shalom that also intersects with your passion/interests?

For this "participate and enrich" aspect of missionary posture to become truly activated within the body of Christ, churches must find ways to communicate the value of what members are doing in their worlds outside the church. For example, when measuring how actively engaged members are in the life of the church, do pastors count what their people are doing in God's name outside the doors of the church? Too often, churches gauge ministry success with metrics that only include participation in defined church programs, ministries and events. By leaving out the profiling of day-to-day connections and service opportunities members have with everyday people, pastors unintentionally suggest that activities outside the reach of the church's organized ministries aren't that important. And they also miss the opportunity to highlight "wins" for the body of Christ that are happening nearly every day.

Churches also need to find creative ways to keep their missional priorities operable against the other demands of wider discipleship. For example, it is worth the effort for churches to prioritize discovery activities aimed at finding out what good initiatives the city or neighborhood has already sanctioned to enrich the local community. This knowledge is critical because such civic programs often present opportunities for the Church to join in and serve alongside non-Christians, while also communicating to the city that the Church can be about no-strings-attached service. In short, church leaders need to resist the natural urge to create a Christian version of what is already happening locally. This often unwisely depletes churches of energy and resources, and church-sourced initiatives frequently make it harder or undesirable for non-Christian neighbors to be involved.

Of course, there are clearly times when it is most appropriate for local churches to create or join Christian-based initiatives. For example, in my own city, Imago Dei Church has started the "Advent Conspiracy." The idea is that if we reduce what we normally spend on Christmas gifts and consuming, and we invest the savings in good causes (e.g. drilling wells in areas that face crises related to potable water shortages), we in Christ's name can change the world for good. The Advent Conspiracy has become not only a powerful shalom-sowing initiative across the Portland area; many hundreds of churches across the nation have now adopted this same program, and waves of goodness are going out all over the world that bless many in Jesus' name!

Selecting a small subset of missional trajectories out of a broad spectrum of opportunities requires church leadership teams to practice communal discernment as the logical outflow of missionary absorbing, relating and serving. Just as individuals must make choices about where to invest their missional passions, churches must also be wise about what they can realistically take on. An activist approach that disregards the necessity of good boundaries and discerning choices is the recipe for low impact, and even burnout, over the long haul.

Whether we discern it best to join something that is already underway, or whether we decide it is best to create something that is missing, we act and pray and hope that sustainable missional community might emerge. Such communities provide an ideal context for the gospel to be demonstrated and experienced. And they provide excellent belonging spaces for Christians and non-Christians alike to sow shalom together and experience a key aspect of what it means to live a Jesus-life.

EPILOGUE

I believe God is calling Christians everywhere—in their own self-discerned way(s) and consistent with the rhythms most complementary to their design and context—to practice a missionary lifestyle. This is not a part of Christian formation that we can give token attention to, while farming most of it out to the few professional missionaries, apostles, and evangelists in our midst. Rather, it involves each of us embracing a new identity and owning our personal and collective missionary vocation as agents of shalom.

As we wear the mantle of a new identity in the world, we face the challenge of helping one another take the practical steps needed to activate that identity into an actual lifestyle.

Through teaching and demonstrating the pattern I have described, many church leaders are seeing a rising number of their people engaging their cities as missionaries of God's shalom. The behaviors associated with that pattern come from observing the people of God, historically (the exiles in Babylon), and presently (my own experience and that of many others as missionaries crossing cultural boundaries to convey the good news). They constitute three dynamic and overlapping couplets of behavior: immerse and listen; connect and befriend; and participate and enrich. And they are learned and practiced in a way of life that continually stays tuned into God's presence and discerned purposes, all the while behaving in ways that humbly honor the Lord's work ahead of us and his desire to use our lives to proclaim his wonderful good news. (Note: I include in Appendix B a tight summary of ways to explain this pattern, including some representative questions for people to wrestle with in order to comprehend the significance of each couplet of behavior).

Through small group settings, church planter assessments, training intensives, one-on-one coaching, and sermons every now and then, my wife and I have been giving ourselves to helping our fellow Christians embrace and activate their call to be local missionaries.[26] As we pass the baton of these concepts and practices on to others, we are seeing some pretty amazing stories of change in and through the lives of people who have been living inside the bubble of the American Christian subculture. I do not believe there is a "best" or singularly "optimal" way to engage the Church and move her into her missional calling, but I do believe we have to start somewhere. I propose this perspective and practical missionary lifestyle as one way to get the flywheel in motion.

I hope that you will be inspired to give the missionary identity and lifestyle a "go" in your own journey with Christ and with your church. It is consistent with that Great Commission given us by the Prince of Shalom, Jesus Christ, to "go and

---

26 In our Portland context this presently involves collaborating with Forge America (www.forgeamerica.com) and Christian Associates (www.christianassociates.org) to develop "ForgePDX," a missional hub for training, coaching, and mobilizing missional pioneers and church planters. It also includes running missional small groups (we call them "good-newsing groups"), and I have included an overview of such a group in Appendix C.

make disciples of the nations" (Matt 28:18-20). It falls within the vein of that call to live shrewdly and actively engage the world God loves as "salt and light" agents who press into the tension of living "in the world but not of it" (Matt 5:19-22; John 17). And it is a call that each of us can assume, with an assurance of a degree of success, for we have the power of the Holy Spirit breathed upon us and in us to enable us to fruitfully sow shalom and Good News (John 20:23). May God give us the grace to respond, for his glory and for the good of the world!

BIBLIOGRAPHY

Brueggemann, Walter. *Living Toward a Vision: Biblical Reflections on Shalom*. Cleveland: The Pilgrim Press, 1982.

DeVries, Dave. "The Challenge of Engaging Culture." *Missional Challenge*, March 4, 2008. No pages. Online: http://www.missionalchallenge.com/2008/03/challenge-of-engaging-culture.html.

Hirsch, Alan. *The Forgotten Ways: Reactivating the Missional Church*. Grand Rapids: Brazos, 2009.

Leithart, Peter J. *Defending Constantine: The Twilight of an Empire and the Dawn of Christendom*. Downers Grove: IVP Academic, 2010.

Lenzner, Robert and Johnson, Stephen S. "Seeing Things as They Really Are." *Forbes*, March 10, 1997. No pages. Online: http://www.forbes.com/forbes/1997/0310/5905122a.html.

Maynard, Brother. "Missional Order: Shalom." *Subversive Influence,* October 30, 1997. No pages. Online: http://subversiveinfluence.com/2007/10/missional-order-shalom/.

Murray, Stuart. *Post-Christendom: Church and Mission in a Strange New World (After Christendom)*. Milton Keynes: Paternoster, 2004.

Plantinga, Cornelius. *Not the Way It's Supposed to Be: A Breviary of Sin*. Grand Rapids: Eerdmans, 2010.

Reagan, David. "The Lion and the Lamb." *Learn the Bible.* No pages. Online: http://www.learnthebible.org/the-lion-and-lamb.html.

van Steenwijk, Mark. "Incarnational Practices." *Next-Wave Church & Culture*, October 2005. No pages. Online: http://outwardthinking.com/thenextwave/archives/issue85/index-63885.cfm.html.

Weston, Paul. *Lesslie Newbigin: Missionary Theologian*. Grand Rapids: Eerdmans, 2006.

Wright, Christopher J.H. *The Mission of God: Unlocking the Bible's Grand Narrative*. Downers Grove: IVP Academic, 2006.

———. "Prophets to the Nations." *Encounters Mission Journal*. 29(9). No pages. Online: http://www.redcliffe.org/SpecialistCentres/EncountersMissionJournal/vw/1/ItemID/54.

Wright, N.T. *Surprised by Hope: Rethinking Heaven, the Resurrection, and the Mission of the Church*. New York: HarperCollins, 2009.

Yoder, John Howard. *For the Nations: Essays Evangelical and Public*. Grand Rapids: Eerdmans, 1997.

APPENDICES

APPENDIX A

Listening and Learning In Context via "Neighborhood Exegesis"

Aim of Exercise: to give participants a hands-on experience of the power of missionary listening in particular areas or neighborhoods in their city; and to build on that toward a deeper embedding and expressing of the gospel.

What is "neighborhood exegesis" and why is it important?

Exegesis = reading out—A fancy theological term describing the activity of digging into the:
- background
- history
- ethos
- literary context
             ... of a passage of Scripture

"Neighborhood Exegesis" = digging into the:
- background
- history
- ethos
- contextual issues

What's really here is reading out of context. It is not like demographic studies unattached to real relationships or involving minimal relational investment. But it is a means by which a church or aspiring church plant can increase its awareness and responsiveness to those it is called to reach/serve.

It is important because it: helps us discern where God is at work; enhances our awareness (stewardship); helps us respond to need and potential; fuels prayer and the ministry of "peripateo"... and it is fun for team building!

How do we conduct a listening exercise?

1. Select locale and time when residents are home.
2. Gather for initial connecting/instructions—review why we're doing this and pray.
3. Send groups of 2-3, with maps, and hand out questions.
4. Groups interact as they observe ... then perform 3 actions (on the handout).
5. Re-convene and debrief observations and experiences.
6. Brainstorm and process questions.
7. Have an "insider" respond to the observations.

Sample of an actual listening exercise:

8:45 am – Arrivals at Cedar Mill Church (over muffins and pastries and coffee)

9:00–9:15 am – Dan explains the exercise, assigns groups and target zones with maps

9:15–10:45 am – Groups travel to and walk designated areas and answer the questions

10:45 am – 12:00 pm – Debrief the exercise together, with each group sharing its   insights and a story about the token/symbol they collected. A guest or participant who lives in the zone shares their own account of the context as a wrap up to the story-sharing about relics.

12:00 pm – Dan prays to close the morning.

Questions to aid our listening to the soundings of context:

We're going to take time observing and learning a bit about a part of our city. As we walk and observe and listen in groups of 2-4 people, the questions below will help us see and experience our city in new ways.[27] They will also hopefully help inform our understanding of and responsiveness to the neighborhoods and social groupings in this particular area. We will end by reflecting on what it might mean to seek the shalom of these places (Jer. 29:7).

- As you stand at your starting point this morning, what do you see as you look in each direction? What do you hear or sense? What activity do you notice?

As you begin to walk about ...

- What do you notice about the front yards or entries to each of the houses or apartments?
- Does this neighborhood or part of the city feel like a cared-for place?
- How many houses, apartments or buildings for sale do you see? What indicators of transience do you observe?
- Where you see a park, what do you notice about it? Does it feel like an inviting place? Who is there?
- Do you pass any churches or religious buildings? What does their appearance communicate to you?
- What kinds of commercial buildings are there? Who makes up the clientele?
- How many people do you see walking about or tending to their homes/yards or businesses? What age, race, and gender are they?
- How pedestrian-friendly is this place of the city? Are there sidewalks, lights, or crosswalks?

---

27 These questions are permutations of a set Bakke Graduate University and others have devised.

- Are there places in this area or neighborhood that you would not go into? Why?
- Where are the places of life, hope, beauty, or community in this particular area or neighborhood?
- What evidence of struggle, despair, neglect, and alienation do you see?
- In what ways do you sense God's presence in this area?

NOTE: *Along the way:* 1) Talk to someone; 2) Drink something at a local hangout; and 3) Bring back a token, a symbol that captures your experience of the community.

DEBRIEFING ...

1. First ask: *What did I notice in myself—thoughts, strong feelings or reactions, etc., as I absorbed what I saw and experienced?*

2. Groups share one at a time about the "soundings" they picked up from the area they traversed ...

   How were your observations similar? How were they different?

3. Process:
   - *What signs of shalom or the Kingdom do you see here (i.e., where God seems to already be at work)?*

   - *What might it look like to "seek the shalom" of this sector of the city? In other words, how might I join others in ministering and enriching this area?*

     Derivative to this: *What forms of church are needed here that are not represented in the current churches?*

   - *Any early thoughts on what your church or church plant might do to enhance its overall listening in context?*

4. Have a resident of the area respond to the observations and fill-out the story of the area.

APPENDIX B

Representative Questions for Each Couplet of Missionary Behavior

Immerse and Listen

Involves indwelling as a "participant observer," seeking to get below the surface to really understand our context, including its history. The immersion process includes getting to know the social rhythms of people living in our area, as well as listening to their stories, hopes, fears, laments, biases and values (both expressed and observed in the way they live). It also involves exploring the good that people are up to on a communal level, and identifying needs that are apparently unaddressed. All along we're listening to the spiritual soundings—how do people view Christians and the church, what sins are apparent and what stands in the way of people accepting the gospel, and most importantly, where does God already seem to be at work?

What are the key questions and issues that people repeatedly bring up when you ask them about what concerns them?

What seems to be good news to those God has called us to be among? (i.e. discover what residents see as good news, before getting into sharing The Good News of Christ).

What do they view as bad news, and where have you personally been impacted by the lament, pain or sins of the neighborhood?

Connect and Befriend

Involves establishing relational proximity with locals so that no-strings-attached friendships are cultivated over time, in the hope that we might live and naturally share Jesus and his good news along the way. This includes joining and/or establishing various affinity groups, with/among non-Christians in our context, that intersect with natural areas of interest we have (e.g., sports teams, yoga classes, classes, etc.). It also involves inhabiting popular community spaces ("third places") where locals hang out. All along we as Christ-followers take into account that people often need to belong and serve constructively alongside us before they actually come to believe what we believe.

How do you yourself build friendships with non-Christians?

How do you and your church create belonging spaces for non-Christians open to spirituality but not open to coming to a worship gathering?

Participate and Enrich

Involves coming along existing shalom-sowing initiatives that (ideally) coincide with our own passions and spiritual convictions. These may be sourced within the church, or they may be initiatives started by people or organizations outside the church. We serve and move into various causes in the hope that missional communities might be birthed that include a rich blend of Christians and non-Christians. In our participation in culture, we are not simply trying to be missionaries who embed in the subcultures of our city. We are aiming to be missionaries who pray for, provoke and bring shalom.

How might your natural passions and interests intersect with mission?

What one area and/or sphere of relationship might you join others in to sow shalom in your city?

APPENDIX C

Learning how to be Missionaries in SE Portland

Catching the vision to follow Jesus outside the walls of the church ...

> Build houses and settle down; plant gardens and eat what they produce. Marry and have sons and daughters; find wives for your sons and give your daughters in marriage, so that they too may have sons and daughters. Increase in number there; do not decrease. Also, seek the peace and prosperity of the city to which I have carried you into exile. Pray to the LORD for it, because if it prospers, you too will prosper.' - Jeremiah 29:1-7 (NIV)

> Seek the shalom of the city where I have sent you into exile, and pray to the Lord on its behalf, for in its shalom you will find your shalom.

What's this small group about? An 8-week group experience where we'll share and stimulate one another to demonstrate and bring God's shalom to our neighborhoods, workplaces and social networks? We'll start each evening with a simple soup meal at the Steigerwalds' home, then we'll have lively conversations about how to live naturally as missionaries right here in Portland (see sample themes below, plus group meeting times).

Prerequisites: Openness to God and a commitment to come to all Tuesday evening sessions. Background reading: *Tangible Kingdom Prime*r, by Hugh Halter and Matt Smay

Our Starting Schedule:

Oct 2 – Catching the vision to follow/find Jesus outside the walls of the church

Oct 9 – Learning to behave like missionaries in Portland

Oct 13 – Neighborhood listening experience together (it's fun!)

Oct 30 - What initiatives might we create or join to enrich our local context?

Nov 6 – How do we befriend normal people and create belonging spaces for them?

Nov 13 – What is this good news we bring?

Nov 20 – What does proclaiming the gospel look like today?

Nov 27 – How can we grow in Christ-likeness and discernment amid mission?

Dec 4 - What does it mean to "live prophetically" (in contrast to culture)?

Dec 11 – What have we learned and how can we pass it on?

ABOUT THE AUTHOR

Dan Steigerwald lives in Portland Oregon with his Canadian wife of 25 years, Ann. Prior to settling in Portland, he served 20 years in Europe and various developing world contexts as a missionary, church-planter, and pastor. Dan is a longstanding active leader in Christian Associates International (http://christianassociates.org), and leads coaching teams with Bridges (www.bridgesus.org) and George Fox Seminary (where he earned a DMin in Leadership in the Emerging Culture and now serves as an Adjunct Professor). He loves helping leaders and churches develop and implement missional training and church planting strategies, while also advocating for various creation care and shalom-sowing initiatives in his neighborhood and city. Dan can be reached at dlsteigerwald@gmail.com.

ABOUT
URBAN LOFT PUBLISHERS

Urban Loft Publishers focuses on ideas, topics, themes, and conversations about all things urban. Renewing the city is the central theme and focus of what we publish. It is our intention to blend urban ministry, theology, urban planning, architecture, urbanism, stories, and the social sciences, as ways to drive the conversation. We publish a wide variety of urban perspectives, from books by the experts about the city to personal stories and personal accounts of urbanites who live in the city.

OTHER BOOKS BY ULP

Text & Context: Church Planting in Canada in Post-Christendom
Leonard Hjalmarson, Editor

Chapter Contributors: Jamie Arpin-Ricci, Sean Benesh, Robert Cameron, Nathan Colquhoun, Scott Cripps, Laurence East, Frank Emmanuel, David Fitch, Phil Harbridge, Jamie Howison, Rob Laidlaw, Kim Reid, Robb Scott, Dan Steigerwald. Foreword by well known pastor Bob Roxburgh and afterword by Scott Hagley of Forge Canada.

How does the text of the gospel take root in a post-Christendom culture? What sort of disciplines and imagination root a kingdom presence in Canadian neighbourhoods? How does this frame of "church plant" shift in our renewed awareness of the missio Dei? This project tells the stories of eleven church planters, in nine Canadian cities. In part, it comprises a research project to discover what stories are really being written on the Canadian front lines. It anticipates a diverse contextualization of the gospel as we re-enter the neighbourhoods of towns and cities and urban centers.

Tradecraft: For the Church on Mission
Larry McCrary, Caleb Crider, Wade Stephens, and Rodney Calfee.

The Western Church world is abuzz with talk of being missional. Church leaders, conference speakers, and authors are weighing the merits of the attractional church movement of the past few decades, and where they find it lacking, prescribing changes in the way we need to approach our cultures with the Gospel. There has been a consensus shift among many churches, networks, and denominations to become more focused on mission. The result is a renewed interest in reaching the lost in our cities and around the world. The Church, in many places in the Western world, is in fact returning to a biblical missional focus.

Yet there is something still to be addressed in the process: the how. For centuries, God has called missionaries to cross cultures with the Gospel, and along the way, they have developed the necessary skill-sets for a cultural translation of the Good News. These skills need to be shared with the rest of the Church in order to help them as well be effective missionaries. *Tradecraft: For the Church on Mission* does exactly that. This book, in essence, pulls back the curtain on tools once accessible only to full-time Christian workers moving overseas, and offers them to anyone anywhere who desires to live missionally.

14786326R00061

Made in the USA
San Bernardino, CA
10 September 2014